Englaland

Englaland
Steve Ely

STACK
BOOKS

Smokestack Books
1 Lake Terrace, Grewelthorpe, Ripon HG4 3BU
e-mail: info@smokestack-books.co.uk
www.smokestack-books.co.uk

Englaland

ISBN 978-0-9929581-4-5

Smokestack Books is represented
by Inpress Ltd

I suppose every boy wants to help his country in some way or other.

R.S.S. Baden Powell,
Scouting for Boys

Contents

The Battle of Brunanburh

The past is never dead.
It's not even past.

William Faulkner,
Requiem for a Nun

I

From banks of turbid Rother, mucky suds foaming
on the autumn spate, through fretwork of
osier and screening bulrush, I saw sword-
edge strike and shield-wall splinter, on the
heath at Brunanburh.

Jarls and princes fell, Owein, Strathclyde's King; the
slaughterfield tussocked with dead.

My vision pooled in blood. Garlic thickened in the
bankside silts. Rats plopped, moorhens
scrawked, weasels slunk away: iron set in my
crouching bones.

Sword-slit ship-man crawling in the surge, waxy as
tallow; current whips him away. Dewfall,
blindlight, shouts breaking like stars in the
rout to the river, tumult of thundering
horsethegns.

II

On Weondune, holy hill, grass-slope greased with
   guts, I creep with purse-nets, metal detector,
   the Observer's Book of Bird's Eggs. I peg and
   dig and delve.

Whose is this land? The grass grows brittle on
   leaching bones of Scots; golf club
   groundsmen weed and spray; farmers lurk,
   keepers oil their shotguns.

With needle and cotton, I converted my parka to a
   coat of many pockets; catchstitch,
   backstitch, my *opus anglicanum*. On the
   right-of-way by STRICTLY PRIVATE, I slip
   away quickly, ignoring shouts and raking
   torchbeams. Partridge-pearled, furred with
   coneys, lining full of coin: Æthelstan, *Rex
   totius Britanniae*.

III

That day the cows were restless. We were up near
      the Ship, spinning for pike, when they
      started their urgent lowing. They jostled
      behind us before launching for the river,
      tipping Tosh and his tackle into the herded
      flow. They hauled out on the bank and
      shook like dogs.

A puce-faced farmer came with a bobby and tore
      up our day tickets; some lads had killed a
      calf with idlebacks. We packed up our
      tackle, waited hours in the sun at Ulleskelf
      station.

Scots and ship-men threw down their weapons and
      leapt into the stream. I watched them
      founder from the crown of a bankside alder.

IV

Bank-earth colour of beaver's pelt, pocked with
      holes. Under fringing sod, above the
      kingfisher's oozing cloaca – spaced oblongs
      of martins. Waterline, rat tunnels, hand-
      holds for drowners, dragged down by
      floodsurge   and   grappling   fingers,
      backspeared by point-blank javelins.

The horsemen wheeled for Brynes Ford; gravels
      choked with corpses, festive with looters.

V

We whetted our blades on Harthill scythe-stone
and mounted for slaughter. Hoof-splash
streaked our backs with blood.

Stragglers at Guilthwaite; we cut them down. Spoil
there was for taking, cruxata of Dublin
swords, their stinking pelts of mail.

Remembering our dead, we pruned noses, clipped
genitals, rode garlanded in ears.

Morthen, the *thyng* on the *moor*, witan of shaken
spears. Alternatively, 'slaughterplace', *Ding's
Mere* by metathesis.

There breathless pause for bearings. Duskfall,
fuming rain, columns from the east; the
sound of distant horses. The nailed fleet
moored at Castleford. A night and a day,
polaris and sol, cross surgent rivers, through
forest and fen, past spoilgreedy hamlets of
English and Dane.

Nape hairs lifting. Snipe tear up from floodfield,
panicking greylags honk aloft; drumbeat of
horses, clash of swords unsheathing –

A stump-cross sings the slaughter, foamed in
wreathy pignut, beside the Primitive
Methodist church.

VII

The King's endowment: lauds in the forest chantry. Plainsong of blackbird and contrapuntal thrush; earthworm and landsnail, the cantarists' perpetual stipends.

I rose with the song and arranged my relics: the osteoporosis femur from the graveyard of St. Lawrence; the blue stone from the roman road; skulls of hare and roadkill badger, bastard-wings of jays; magpie piety, tongue-tied cult of saints.

Bryony's scarlet beads, Our Father, Hail Mary. Rood of corky elder, apocryphal scoring in the beech bole's elephant folio. Pray for the dead, for God's anointed, Ælfric and Æthelwin, earls and sons of kings.

I tracked them from Rother in hope of plunder,
skulking in ditches and gullies of streams.

The lopped-limb Hansel and Gretel trail, flocked
with corvids. Blindman's bushcraft.

Ravenfield: 'the place where the northmen raised
their raven banner'. The glib derivations of
amateurs.

The tenner worked free from the drunk's back-
pocket and drifted to the pavement; I bent
to my laces, palmed narwhal dagger, struck
coins of Novgorod.

IX

Daybreak. We crept from under gorse and looked
down upon another brown river: Danube,
Dnieper – *Don*. A line of ant-men wading
the ford. We nosed the breeze, confirmed
the horsemen absent.

We breasted the waters, emerged sopping onto
sands. Bone-numb, chatter-teeth cold. I bent
and retched.

The cloud-smeared sun confirmed the street's
direction. We joined stragglers striding
north, soft boots slopping and squelching.

X

Woodsmoke in the forest. We unsheathed our
swords and strode into a farmyard,
scattering chickens, holding curs at bay.

A girl there spoke our language, or near enough.
We wolfed bread and hot pottage, paid in
Varangian coin.

We tracked them to Ryknild, the ridge between the
rivers, and rode them down.

They drew half-hearted swords, then stumbled for
the kjarr. No stomach for fight, no legs for
flight.

We verged the street with dead. Little resistance,
less spoil; they'd peeled their mail in the
night.

Beyond was Dearne-ford and a day's trek to their
ships. The lads gave up the pursuit; they had
nothing left worth taking. Besides, past
Bodeltone, Danes had settled; you never
knew whose side those bastards were on.
They turned back. I pressed on for glory.

XII

Sheffield and Hallamshire Cup, September, '85.
        Away to The Gate, at Swinton. We got beat,
        nine-nowt. They had back-perms and their
        thighs glistened with oil. We had bed-hair
        and beer-guts.

We drowned our sorrows in the Sandygate Hotel,
        where the bandit went haywire and kept
        paying out. We dropped thirty quid in
        tokens, cashed them in for Ayingerbrau.

Some galloned-up yokels offered us out. Ginner
        got jumped in the bogs. We grappled our
        way back to the car.

We pulled over at Bolton bridge, lined up and
        pissed into the stream.

XIII

Riders fell on us from nowhere. We dived into fen
  and prostrated in the reeds. Coots and
  dabchicks squealed. I breathed black water.

We bellied to the ford, flushing rails and bitterns
  before us. A horseman waited on the gravels.
  Estrith broke cover and ran. A spear passed
  through him. I dropped to my knees and
  lied in order to live.

At South Pump wood, big lads pinned me down.
Armed with egg-shampoo, the typewriter,
one-in-the-face-or-ten-in-the-stomach,
they began their leisured torture.

Raw with burns, I bargained to save my skin;
offered bullfinch egg, catapult, what was left
of a quarter of midget gems.

Big ants and baby elephants paraded on my
ribcage, twigs teased snot from my bloody
nose; they made me eat it, wrote *fuk of* on
my forehead in permanent marker.

XV

A hoard in the ash at Holy Well, he said, relics from
the east: a nail from the true cross, the
vinegar sponge, the spearhead of Longinus;
marvellous treasures, my King would
reward me greatly. His eyeballs darted like a
viper's tongue – *he had nothing.* I looped
rope around his neck and bade him lead.

Kestrel's nest swung it. Collar-gripped, hand-cuffed, hobbled by Doc Mart arsebones, I feigned abjection and tensed for the moment. I led them under the railway and pointed to the tree – *that's it, in that old maggy's* – and tore myself free.

Panic whirred my legs bionic; I sprinted the cornfield, leapt the dike, crashed through the Plantation and scrambled to the summit of Broad Lane tips, where Curts and Cyril were waiting.

At the foot of the hundred-foot incline, they gave up the chase, hawking and phlegging, brushing caked-clay from the flares of their catalogue Falmers.

They sparked up Number Sixes and roared how they'd kill us. We told them, *Come on then you bastards!* And legged it over the tips when they made as if they would.

I knew that tree; I knew them all. The Well-Bred
Oaks at Ringstone Hill, the Gospel Thorn,
the crab-tree haired in hoary lichen …

*Too obvious, the ancient ash right next to Oswald's
well. Likely this English knew the land like the
back of his hand …*

What would I do? …

*A furlong in front, the pilgrimless well, the life-tree
looming. I grabbed the rope and pulled…*

Knotted together, we brawled in the clay. I gripped
his knife-hand. He bit my wrist. I kneed him
in the face. He wrapped his thighs around
my neck and tried to snap me. I back-flipped
free and pulled hard upon the rope …

*I looked up and watched him transform into a vargr,
black eyes burning, curling lips, revealing
slavering fangs …*

That hollow tree was empty. I sucked the poison
from my veins and kicked him in the head
as I walked back to the horse.

XVIII

When hoof-fall frittered to silence, I stood up from
the bracken. The ship-man fought like a
snared wolf, but in the end, succumbed. I
cut him naked with his own black dagger.
His ribs revealed like the planks of a ship.
His swan-white skin was bruised like a seed-
bean.

His coin purse was empty. I pressed my fingers
along the seams of his shirt, touch-mining
for amber or eastern emeralds – flushing
nought but ticks and flat-lice. I dug a hole
by the well and cairned him with the wild
stones of the field. Don't ask me why.

XIX

I came round to gurgles, the grunting of the byre.
    A gurning simpleton grinned into my face.

He led me to a barn with a litter of patchy whelps.
    He handed them to me, cooing and purring,
    slobbering drool from his fungus mouth.
    We petted them together.

I gestured for food. He showed me a sweetcrab
    laden with fruit, returned with bread and
    ale. I ate and felt some strength return.

He led me to stepping-stones over a river, a hilltop
    henge, an oak tree blasted by lightning. A
    way-cross by the Roman road.

I broke from his grip and began the long march
    north. He clung to me, griping and wailing.
    I smashed him down, finished him with a
    stone.

XX

I could never decide: Christ crucified, or the one-
eyed god of the gibbet.

Stone circle on the hill, wreathed with wraiths and
weirds of Welsh. I went there to be shriven.
Face down in leafy trefoil, I offered
expiation, wergild for the soul.

Ravens cawed from the rune-scored bluestones;
God's stroffage deemed my coin debased.

Now from the sixth hour there was darkness over all the land and the Good Friday feast on the common began.

Those that smashed the bluestones clove to their lightless altars with wailing and gnashing of teeth, as domestics and milkmaids cavorted with farmhands and flat-capped colliers; hook-a-duck, cocks-and-hens, hoopla and beer stalls; shagging on the bracken-bank down by Grimey Dell.

A Benidorm generation let it slip away: Vauxhall Vivas, bungalows, Coronation Street. The immemorial nine acre arena, blowing with rape, rootless hedgerows of etherised Japanese knotweed.

XXII

At a cross-hill by an ancient yew, I stumbled on
      comrades, bathing in a spring. Scabbed and
      hobbled, a sorry bunch, they marvelled at
      my chest rosette, the rip-hole in my back. A
      half day's march to the mudbanked fleet. We
      straggled along in threes and fours, sharing
      stories of the war. Even in defeat, a man can
      find glory, a song to sing in hall.

XXIII

We took a riotous hundred from Elmsall and
Kirkby, tooled-up with golf-clubs, brush
handles, bars; because they brayed Steve
Burgin in the market bus stop. We cleared
the streets, filled-in some lads at Vale Head
Park.

See-you-Jimmae! Jocks jumped us on the lines at
Hague Hall Hill, hailing half-bricks,
shouting and bawling in their on-and-off
Scotch Estate accents. We routed them up
the tips; cop-cars came; Mongol got arrested.
Break-time bards immortalised the story,
the deeds of Daz, of Pat and Cooky, the
legend of Arthur Wakefield.

XXIV

Pogged with plunder, glutted with glory, I turned
    back for the tented-field.

Bone-beat, sinew-sore, I slumped in the saddle,
    nodding like the horse.

A furlong before me, a boy slunk in shadow.
    Seeking company, I hailed him, to regale
    with tales, keep my lids from dropping shut.

He leapt like a hare and fled into forest.

XXV

Rule number one: when in a foreign land or nesting up Frickley Park, hide on sight of strangers.

Rule number two: when in a foreign land or nesting up Frickley Park, flee if strangers hail to parley.

Rule number three: when in a foreign land or nesting up Frickley Park, take ten or a dozen, deputy's sticks, the Cock of the School, if possible.

Black Jacks, crow's egg, a marbled penknife; Dublin coin, carved walrus blades, a lock of salt-bleached hair: what's mine stays mine.

XXVI

We fell on them in their cells in the eremitic wood;
    the cult of St. Oswald, another would-be
    Bretwalda. We garrotted them with their
    rosaries, out of spite, mostly. With us, Christ
    was ever, only skin-deep.

XXVII

Return journeys always seem shorter. Dearne, Don
and Rother, wolves and white-tailed eagles,
tidying the trail.

Weondune, a feast in preparation: the spit and
crack of poleroast pigs, stewards staggered
under weight of swollen aleskins.

Churls dug graveholes, noble bodies burned.
Laughter and cheering, eulogies for the
dead. Riches. I leapt from the horse and
roared my arrival.

XXVIII

We were among the last. The Scots had sailed
already. A captain counted me one of twenty
five. We shouldered the snekkja into the
flow and hauled aboard. We scabbarded our
swords and oared for Humber.

XXIX

A box lid filled with flour, blown eggs arranged in
    size: jenny wren to waterhen.

Tutankhamen's shattered capo-di-monte treasure,
    fished from Langthwaite Beck, stashed
    shards in a paint-can in Wack's backyard ...
    hey yeah, from when he invaded England ...
    hey yeah, the Green Hills were his pyramids
    ...hey yeah, that cable bobbin was a chariot
    wheel ...

Burdock-bundled, withy-wired, cached in loamy
    woodsoil; a boy's booty, microcosmic jewels
    of jays.

XXX

I made my excuses and retired to my pavilion, to
   curl up with a book: Fitter & Richardson,
   Pocket Guide to British Birds; the Anglo-
   Saxon Chronicle.

From under the blowing dolmen, I looked down
   on Hall Steads and beyond to the Park
   Springs Business Park and saw England for
   the first time: arable carucates watered with
   blood, oxgangs limed with ribcage and
   femur.

The hillstones rang with song; croaks of crakes and
   foaming bustards, anthems for Æthelstan,
   King. Larks rose from the corn and
   thundered their exult vision: this land lives
   and its dead cannot die.

Scum of the Earth
A Play in One Act

Dramatis Personae

Arthur Wellesley, Field Marshall His Grace the First Duke of
Wellington

Peter Benjamin, The Right Honourable Lord Mandelson of Foy
in the County of Hereford, and Hartlepool in the County of
Durham

A Chorus of the Swinish Multitude

*St. Crispin's Day, the playing fields of Eton (Towton, Orgreave, St.
Peter's Field) before a momentous battle in a second English Civil
War. On opposite sides of the battlefield, the two generals,
Wellesley and Mandelson, rally their troops before the
commencement of hostilities.*

Wellesley:
    Fighting men of England! Bind on your braces,
    brush down your Ben Shermans, double-knot
    the laces of your oxblood DMs; unsheath
    kukris, stilettos and samurai swords,
    carving knives lifted from cutlery drawers;
    grip numchucks, shillelaghs and Louisville Sluggers,
    coshes, axe-handles, spring-loaded batons;
    rack the slides of your Glocks and Berettas,
    flick to full auto MAC 10s and AKs;
    load milk crates with molotovs,
    line up kerb stones and half-bricks –

Mandelson:
    Peashooters and stink bombs, cattys and claysticks,
    Air Bomb Repeaters and knock-a-door-run.
    Really! So these are the English, are they,
    hemispheric lords shrunk to small-arms

vigilantes, a sink estate legion
of ASBO louts and beer-can boors, chips and guacamole
scratch card monkeys? They'd swing in Foy,
make no mistake – a fair trial of course,
judged and juried by my peers. Look at them,
their shaven heads and tattoos, their trademark infringing
Hong Kong Lacoste; listen to them; dropped aitches,
soccer chants and estuary *innit*,
inelecute provincial demotic:
in the words of the poet, *thick as fuck,*
common as muck – pardon my French. Not so much
a people's army as a hooligan mob,
Carling-fuelled, set out to raze
a paedophile's home. And this, in a nutshell,
is what is at stake. To whom belongs the future?
To whom belongs the land? Who will rule, we, or they –

A Swine:

Us, you posh cunt –

Mandelson:

Yet I assert 'we'. Consumers and customers,
stakeholders in the United Kingdom
of Great Britain and Northern Ireland PLC,
our European and International partners
and friends; I am privileged to address you
at this moment of moment, on which the destiny
of our One World will turn. Across this staked arena,
beyond the whitewashed rugby posts, our enemy awaits:
the English, a steaming ruck of gougers
and maulers, rakers and brawlers, captained
by a dead man, playing a dead man's hand.
Flying St. George and Plantagenet lions
they imagine they can be a nation again.
Yet I tell you these standards shall be their shrouds.
The days of this nation are no more;
those who once were mighty, are now among
the wretched of the earth, doled and dispossessed,

casualised into call centres
and regional distribution hubs,
zero-hour contracts and flexible working,
sedated, if not sedate, on *Eastenders*,
X Factor, Sky Sports and Lambrini.
How they live, these illiterate troglodytes,
this ignoble white trash, this tabloid-whipped
scum of the earth –

Wellesley:
Hear the man; how he sees you: do you
recognise yourselves? Well, take a look
in the mirror, at your trackies and trainers
and Superdry tat, the laughing stock
of the Paris catwalks. Look at yourselves,
five bellied on lager and Southern Fried Chicken,
scorning sea bass, samphire and the eighteen varieties
of balsamic vinegar. Look at yourselves,
reading Chris Ryan and *Heat* magazine,
neglecting Martin Amis, oblivious
to *Granta*. For shame! And how was the Uffizi
this summer? Don't tell me, you went
to 'the Dominican', all-inclusive,
all you could eat, all you could drink, karaoke
Jessie J until the sun came up –

A Swine:
It was fucking brilliant –

Wellesley:
Indeed. And did you speak to the locals
in that charming vernacular? Or *en Español*?
I think we all know the answer to that,
you monoglot barbarians; the world
may be your oyster, but each resort you visit
morphs to Wakefield city centre
on a summer's Saturday night: vomit,
kebabs and riot vans –

A Swine:

Whose side are you on, you Mick bastard? –

Wellesley:

Bear with me, soldier, I'm getting there.
and remember; though a man may be born
in a stable, it doesn't make of him a horse.
So that's what you are, is it? Drunken,
cultureless, belching, farting filth?
Because that's how they see you, those traitors
over there, those Bilderberg 'Brits',
those Sunday supplement Social Democrats,
those *see-you-(in-Tuscany)-Jimmae* London jocks.
What do they know, of your lives and aspirations,
your country and history, the ancient blood
of a fateful people, these fifth column quislings
who sold us to Brussels for peerages, pensions
and Paddington *pieds-a-terre* –

[Cheers from the Swine.]

A Swine:

Pieds-a-terre? Who's he pillocking? He's houses
and mansions all over Europe –

A second Swine:

They all piss in the same pot –

Wellesley:

Was Mandelson at Maldon? Did Blair
at Brunanburh brandish the broadsword?
Did Brown bend the bow at Crecy, Cameron
at Calais? Were McKinsey at Minden
Saatchi at Salamanca, News Corp
with Nelson at Nile? Never! The drumbeat
of blood and fuming cordite sends them jittering
to the jakes and faxing their bankers.
A pox on their pinstriped blue-sky dreams!

Those limp-wrist leeches vision nothing but lucre,
pawning Parliament to Prodi,
racking Runnymede for 'rights', the Shires
slaved with Slavs and mortgaged to Muslims.
Is this the inheritance we wish for our sons?
Is this the England of Maggie and Mafeking,
Waterloo and Winston, Dunkirk and Drake?
Little men, they want you to be *small*,
post-industrial peasants at the pleasure
of their hedge funds, gulled and gullivered
with Romish red tape, the writs and rackets
of race-relations, the relentless
enervations of equal opportunities.
But each Englishman's George in his wyverned world,
though rust only reddens his sword –
until this Sainted day. Men of England!
Unsheath the scabbed-steel war-tooth, grind back
the flame-edged blade! Today will traitors pay,
when bucklers bite and breaking bone,
feed the ravening corpse-field –

[The Swine roar and clash their weapons.]

A Swine:
Get into the fuckers! –

Mandelson:
[Shaking his head.] Need I say more? Berserked like Breivik,
gorgonned in gormless George's jack, monstered
with macho, moronic on magnates, they feed
at fancy's ancient troughs like grey ghosts
gorging virgin-blood to vampire back to life:
confirming only their definitive death.
Maggie. Minden. Maldon. Their past is past,
like sturgeon, Scargill and jobs-for-life:
their future belongs to us –

A Swine:
Job-for-life? I'll have one of those! –

A second Swine:
But not afters at ASOS! –

A third Swine:
Fuck that! –

A fourth Swine:
Or three-twelve at Next –

The first Swine:
Foy! What is it exactly we're fighting for? –

Mandelson:
For what we have. For what will be and is
becoming. For freedom and rights,
from discrimination, to jobs and careers.
For flexible working, suiting women
and families; dignity in diversity,
multi-culture in community, equal rights
for LGBT. World-class education, services
and health care. Look up, look beyond,
face the future that already is upon us;
we live in One World, neither England,
nor Britain, not Europe nor 'The West';
in the twenty-first century these borders
mean nothing. For from Newquay to Newcastle,
London to Leeds, are not Pole and Pakistani,
Indian and Irish, Ghanaian and Greek,
neighboured together on international streets?
And are not our British brightest and best
in skyscrapered skylines from Manhattan
to Manila? Our own universities,
campused with the world? Our business-studied children,
aspiring to millions, in Joburg, Jakarta,
Bahrain? One World, a global, mobile citizenry

united in common humanity only,
ambition and aspiration, dreams
of riches and fulfilment. 'This England'
they dream of, this Hogarthian heritage
of boozing and brawling, Lordshipped landscapes
peasanted with colliers, taverns and terriers
and endless fighting: is it not time
to let it go? iPad supercedes shovel and pick,
Second Life supplants the first. 'This England'!
'This England' is dead: here on this field,
let's bury it –

[Some muted cheers and also consternation among the Swine.]

A Swine:
Joburg and Jakarta? The fuck's he on about? –

A second Swine:
Poles and Pakistanis? Our street's full of them
and it's no better for it –

The first Swine:
Hey lads! Is there 'dignity in diversity'
in the Amazon warehouse? –

A third Swine:
No, but there's equality alright.
'Poles and Pakistanis, Indians and Irish,
Ghanaians and Greeks' – they treat us all like shit –

A second Swine:
I've got a terrier. I drink in 'taverns'.
And I used to be a collier… I think –

The first Swine:
You fucking peasant! Put down your pint
and get with the times. Do something useful
with your life! Show some aspiration,

some initiative, a little en-tre-pre-neu-ri-al spirit;
get yourself an iPad, decamp to Dubai,
hold hands with some shirt-lifting Pakis:
WHY CAN'T YOU JUST BE NORMAL YOU STUPID
ENGLISH CUNT! –

[The Swine laugh uproariously.]

Wellesley:
Indeed. And this is why we fight. England
for the English, Hengist's rough blood
and Conqueror's iron, flowering in the veins
of Edwards, Henrys, ermined Earls,
and cur-dogs of the field –

A Swine:
Does he mean us? –

Wellesley:
No less than in their masters. By hundred
and wapentake, province and shire, it is time
to take back our land. From mastiffed moor
and lurchered ley let hound-voice ring;
let wolfish-woodlands and brock-bored hills
growl with pit-dogs; let metropolitan
streets and precincts holler with the chase, good lads
and brave bitches throwing tongue
in congress, giving good head. Who will withstand
our mongrel-militia? –

A Swine:
There he goes again –

Wellesley:
Our proud pack pressed from pubs and parishes
running the faithless fox to earth.

To each Englishman this duty, sworn to sluice
the suited scum from Eden into Eden's seas.
Fall on them, drive home the cold steel,
into pinko teachers and journalists,
the fifth-column cosmopolitans
of the BBC, the shills of Shengen
in Westminster and Whitehall, the bypass,
windfarm and strip-mall crooks of cronied councils
and chambers of commerce, the human traffickers
of post-imperial guilt, darkening cities
from hysterical Asia, the criminal Caribbean.
Shillinged to the slaughter, pay out in the coin
of the King: spare none and take back our land –

[Muted cheers, bewildered murmurings.]

A Swine:
So, who are we then? The BNP? –

A second Swine:
Alright with me –

A third Swine:
Fuck those bastards, but where are we
when we're done? I've a feeling the cur-dogs'll
be whipped back to their kennels –

The first Swine:
[Nodding in agreement.] In faithful forelock-tugging service,
grateful for slave-slots in service
and social care, freed-up by fucking-up
immigrants –

A second Swine:
Rather us than them –

The third Swine:
'Us' and 'them' puts us all in the poorhouse –

The second Swine:
[Squaring up to the third Swine.] You nigger loving twat!
He's a fucking war hero! –

The third Swine:
So were the Tyneside Irish –

The second Swine:
With the paddies now? Whose side are you on? –

A fourth swine:
NO SURRENDER! –

The third Swine:
They didn't have a chance. German machine guns
cut down all six hundred –

The first Swine:
[Singing.] 'And when the sky darkens and the prospect is war,
who's given a gun and then pushed to the fore
and expected to die for the land of our birth
though we've never owned one lousy handful of earth?' –

The second Swine:
You commie cunt! –

[He lurches forward, throwing haymakers. A brawl ensues and
rapidly spreads through the ranks.]

Mandelson:
[Shaking his head at the commotion, he gestures to his
battalions.]
And there we have it. The England of Scargill
and Ian Stuart Donaldson via F-Troop
and Harry the Dog. Grisly as Griffin,
gruesome as Galloway – dead as Dave Nellist.
Ladies and gentlemen, it's time; curse them,
and have done – a pox on these English

and their septic heritage isle. The world
has turned and the future is on us,
yet here they are, 'two World Wars
and one World Cup' and the interminable
wives of Henry the Eighth. For how much longer
must dead men hold us back? For how much longer
must we wait for plural gay marriage? For how many
more years must we suffer the indignity
of Sterling? Our collective carbon footprint
is per capita far the greatest
of the G12 states, and yet the nimbied Shires
go turbine-less, inert with heritage
and useless hedgerow trees. For shame!
And yet we have so much to celebrate:
bravely we vanquished the dinner-hall
tyranny of chips, banished smokers to the streets
and lawyered the land with alienable 'rights'.
Our world-class universities and incorruptible
academy trusts are the envy of the world,
safeguarded by OFSTED, Fleet Street's finest
and the unsleeping sentinels of the BBC.
Need I even mention the cast-iron
integrity of the City and our blue-chip exports –
global warming, Coldplay, Wallace & Gromit –
and the Lottery-funded talents of our people:
The Voice, Deal or No Deal, Britain's Got Talent!
Colleagues, I believe in you! Let's believe
in ourselves, in each other. Our rainbow
nation can be whatever we want it to be.
Yes we can! –

[The ranks remain restive and brawling. Cat-calls proliferate.]

A Swine:
No we can't. Dole, call centre,
order-picking. They're our options –

A second Swine:
Stop moaning and accept your lot,
you talentless fucker. If you had
anything about you, you'd be a millionaire! –

A third Swine:
We can be whatever we want to be! –

The first Swine:
I'm gonna be an engine driver! –

A fourth Swine:
Astronaut! –

A fourth Swine:
Pirate! –

Wellesley:
Now you're talking, soldier. Every Englishman's
a pirate at heart, from the humblest private
soldier to the Duke of a thousand year name.
Freebooting, fighting and the fancy,
that's our future, not this ball-breaking
bureaucrat vision of boardrooms
and business parks, sistered with sycophants,
sissies and spoilsports. The track and the taproom,
the pit and the pikestaff, Empire's salt-road
of plunder and glory are what we yearn for,
wars, scores and whores, not this piss-poor,
pious penitentiary of chores, bores and snores.
So we fight and we sacrifice, no better
than our fathers. For each man a foaming flagon,
a place of honour at the bar, bread, cheese
and pickles, a haunch of spit-roast boar;
at peddling lathe or puited plough
in quarry and colliery, the khaki
of the King, our dignity and destiny,
this hallowed-hymn we sing. *'And did those feet –*

A Swine:
'The rich man in his castle
The poor man at the gate

[Other swine join in the chorus.]

He made them high and lowly
and ordered their estate.' –

[The swine on both sides erupt in guffawing laughter.]

Wellesley:
[Exasperated.] You plebeian clowns! –

A Swine:
We're clowns alright – and he wants to be
our ringmaster –

A second Swine:
In 'quarry and colliery' – back to the future,
under the overman's whip –

Wellesley:
Jerusalem, damn you! –

The first Swine:
Whose Jerusalem? His landed Lordship's?
The CBI's? What's in it for us?
Knowing our place? Crumbs from the master's table?
For that we're to fight and die? –

A third Swine:
England, their England. A land fit for arseholes –

[Missiles rain in Wellesley's direction and into Mandelson's armies, provoking precipitate skirmishing. Brawling and riot spreads through the ranks of both armies.]

Mandelson:
Fellows! Hold firm! Restrain yourselves –

[He flinches as a turnip flies past his head.]

A Swine:
Next one wins a coconut –

Mandelson:
Colleagues! Friends! Hurl not root-crops at your Lord!
Desist from this unruly squalling!
This is no time to lose our nerve. Our enemies
are in disarray, fighting among themselves
like Millwall at Wembley. Exploit
their disorder; advance and seize the day.
But remember for what we are fighting,
Great Brit – Eng – a world-class, cosmopolitan
country, visioned in glorious aims
and objectives, monitored by milestones
and process ind –

[A second turnip knocks him unconscious. Both armies roar their approval. The missile thrower claps the dirt from his hands.]

A Swine:
That shut the fucker up –

A second Swine:
Good work, brother. Now get in and finish the job –

The first Swine:
What? –

The third Swine:
There's no going back –

The second Swine:
Tyler, Cade, Aske – they failed to press home
their advantage and paid with their lives –

The third Swine:
It's all or nothing. Win the world or die –

The second Swine:
[Fixing bayonet.] Over the top boys! –

[The ranks follow suit and fall on Mandelson and his pinstriped generals.]

Wellesley:
[Spurring his steed and riding along the front line of his riotous, insolent ranks, slashing at them with his riding crop in a vain attempt to quell their insurgency.] Order! Order! Come to order, damn you! The battle is on! Forward! –

[The Boot and Saddle sounds and the battalions lurch forward. Wellesley is engulfed in the riotous crowd and pulled from his horse. He disappears into the melee. The rival armies clash, but after some initial hand-to-hand fighting, seem to realise the futility of their combat and begin to disengage. Soon the fighting is over, and combatants on both sides, recognising their common identity and interests, embrace each other. Some men turn for home, others gather in groups to drink and sing. Some drunken Swine seize the bodies of Mandelson and Wellesley, which they quarter and hang from a tree. As the field straggles to dissolution, sporadic fighting breaks out once more. Beneath the bloody gibbet, a Swine with a guitar sits on the hindquarters of a dead horse and begins to sing.]

A Swine:
Put up the sword
let porter be poured
to toast our accord.

Here's to our health
the old common-wealth
of wood, fen and tilth.

Dog, bitch and pup
lap from the cup
for Jack's game is up.

On Commons and Lords
embezzlers and frauds
shall Ball's wrath be poured.

Tory and Whig
dancing a jig
from Tyburn's rude twig.

Labour's arriviste pimps
gargoyled and gimped
by workers they chimped.

Indentured for wage
the gyrfalcon caged
all Heaven enraged.

With billhook in hand
and cherub's red brand
Adam takes back his land.

Three acres, a cow,
common and plough:
God knows how.

For each man's a whore
the wolf at his door
howling for more.

And George but a shill
for the brutish and shrill
apes of Churchill.

Who keep us irate
on jingo and hate
Empire's dark freight.

Pissers in streams
poisoning dreams
to keep their per diem.

So we freeze in the blare
of headlight glare
like a road-kill hare.

Common

But who will entune a bogged orchard,
Its blossom gone,
Fruit unformed, where hunger and
Damp hush the hive?

Basil Bunting,
Briggflatts

Looking for a Sign on Brierley Common

Looking for a sign on Brierley Common, I found
    not white-tailed eagle, but black-back gulls,
    squalling over ploughland; neither rune nor
    gospel, but the hedge-splayed centrefold of
    Razzle magazine; no hill of blossoming
    maythorn, but a broken pear in a treeless
    orchard.

Lead-legged through brambles and clutching clays,
    steaming in waxy thornproofs, I slogged
    through copse and ditch-banked close,
    looking for a sign; lifting logs and turning
    stones, groping holes in trees; sweat running
    in the sleeves and pooling at the cuffs,
    armpit swelter, eyepits misting; looking for
    a sign –

Chain-ripped sycamores, propped on vermilion
    root discs, wigwammed ready to burn;
    straw-bale hedge-butt, confetti of crimson
    cartridge; lone oak on the Roman road,
    traffic-roar gaining; fag ends, beer cans,
    KFC; looking for a sign –

A heart-shaped rock, dumped ditch-side at
    Ringstone. Rain-rinsed, ploughshare-
    scored, beginning to slime with moss, a
    tongue-tied angel from the mute neolithic.
    Knees buckling, follicles lifting, a beat of
    recognition: *Here am I.* And under the
    pouring sky, furze flamed across the hillside:
    *the place on which thou standest is holy
    ground.*

I flicked off slugs, on drenched grass dragged the earth-side clean. I tried it for weight: a lamped roebuck, a sack of night-bashed spuds. I cradled it like a shotgunned lurcher, and humped it to the van.

Gospel Thorn

I

Holy Thursday on the slope above Tom Bank Wood. Sun beginning to broil in a cloudless galilee sky. Martins wittering psalm-static, flicking for midges over the sherbet rape-field. Yolky scribblers, wheezing their readings from hedgerow lecterns. And the hawthorns transfigured, robed in foamy blossom, enacting their mystery for a vacant congregation.

II

Due west of the Manor, a prominence in the open-field, spring raiment dazzling white – *so then after the Lord had spoken unto them, he was received up into heaven, and sat on the right hand of God* – that men might receive his Spirit, and enter his Kingdom.

III

Rogationtide, the parish in procession, roots as deep as Ryknild: terminalia, ambarvalia, affirming the ancient boundaries, petition for increase in corn and cattle – *thou hast set a bound that they may not pass over; he causeth the grass to grow for kine, and herb for the service of man.* Holy misrule; willow-whips and beer-stops, hymns drunkening to bawdy; the banner of the cross, and that old devil, George's white dragon.

IV

Mark well this land: the oak called Old Adam, where they served bread and cheese; Stumpstone, where parishes meet, where our banner met Kirkby's and the lads spoiled to fight; the Thrashing Post on Ringstone, where if a boy would bear a beating, he might join the men in ale; and the Gospel Thorn above the Dell, where we bowed our heads on Ascension Day, gathered the parish entire.

V

Holy Thursday on the slope above Tom Bank Wood. Ploughed-out, crop-choked, bramble-snagged footpaths. Barbed-wire and threats to prosecute. Farm machines spraying and flailing. Landscape mute and depopulate. But a remnant remains – lampers and moochers, birders and hikers, bluestalkers, dog-walkers, shaggers and gawkers – creedless dissenters from a doped congregation, sleepwalking in the spirit, re-entering their Kingdom.

Eight Miles Out

Eight Miles Out, the in-crowd nite-spot on the glam-rock common, sixty four furlongs equidistant from the coal-fat metropoli of Barnsley, Wakey, Ponty and Donny. No expense spared, sophistication unheard of: phones and lampshades on table-clothed tables, chicken-in-a-basket and Mateus Rose.

They came there every Saturday night, from Elmsall, Kirkby, Moorthorpe and Upton, the ace-face alumuni of missionary Minsthorpe's CSE curriculum: Nick Martin, the platonic form of the boy racer, burning donuts on the gravel in his vinyl-roofed Capri; dodgy Dave Roebuck, hyper on sulphate and money to burn, poppers and porno stashed in his Stag; 'Smooth' Scott Stevens, contemptible shandyman, pulling out of his league in his still hard to credit 911 Turbo; sultry Gail Swanson, slit skirts, basques and twanging suspenders; bouncing Babs Sanders, Jelly-Beaned-easy, spreading her legs on the snail-trail velour; 'Martini' Di Lawrence, anytime/ anywhere nympho slag and back seat blowjob quean.

Eight Miles Out, a house in permanent evolution: Hoyland's short-lived Edwardian retreat, then lodgings for the nurses of the Burntwood sanatorium. '64, named for the plot, the Five Acres Country Club & Casino, and by '79 the tag revived, the Five Acres, an out-of-time dive in breathalysed decline. I was there just once, when a glue-glazed skin stitched me in the bogs and Insane Wayne kicked-off with the bouncers. And for thirty years now, the all-purpose Robin Hood: wedding receptions, family room, grab-a-granny Motown disco every Friday night.

Everything comes and goes; everyone ends up somewhere. Nick Martin sells boats in Brisbane. Dave Roebuck fits carpets somewhere in Donny. Scott Stevens got killed on the North Sea rigs. Gail and Babs married miners, live happy ever after on the Barratt estate. Martini's in London, something or other for Sky TV. Me? I'm eight miles out from nowhere, still hanging around the common.

Dymond's White-tailed Eagle

...þane hasewanpadan,
earn æftan hwit,   æses brucan,
grædigne guðhafoc ...

The Battle of Brunanburh

I

Numb-lipped oxen, mouthing frostbit sod.
Stiffening sheep in hoary bracken. Wasted
deer, nosing from forest onto threadbare
fallows. Starveling English, wraiths of
butchered Norse. Wintry eagle, carrion-
crawed, quartering the common with
salt-bleached, sunlit eye.

II

Perennial rabbits, rats and hedgehogs, pen-released
pheasants, exsanguinated hares. Roadsplat
scribblers, chaffinches, larks. Kamikaze
blackbirds. Remarkable foxes, farm-cats,
stoats; sorrowful owls and hunt-blind
hawks. Once a dog, some mutt stopping
traffic, bright bloods pooling from the split
in its skull. A badger near the fork to
Clayton, proving they were back. The horse
that wrote off the post office van. Stu
Bennett, staggering home from the Nite
Owl. The Mormons thrown from the rolled
Datsun: emergency services, magpies and
crows, quotidian corpse disposal crews.

III

Pole-traps, strychnine, gibbets strung with hook-
      billed vermin. DANGER TO DOGS.
      Shotguns and shillelaghs. Bridewell, assizes,
      eviction and gaol. Holy partridge, sainted
      pheasant. Stuffed behind glass at
      Burntwood Hall, false-eyed *chrysaetos*
      brown: the white-tailed eagle of 1898,
      mantling over a mangy hare. Seen soaring
      over Man-Face Quarry, a sign and a wonder
      for a carrion age, shot on general principle,
      fetched for the Master's praise.

Bomdrop

A droning Dornier, fuming diesel, opened its
bomb-bay short of the pit, straining for
height: TNT tumbled, blasting bedrock
open. That's what it was, this crater in the
arable earth to the west of Barlow's farm: the
Bomdrop. Everyone knew that.

There were no alternative theories. How else to
account for this gouge for no reason, with its
crags of sheer sandstone, fissures and screes?
There we made a tree-swing, piled bales for
cliff-top diving, dug dens in softstone caves.

By middle school, we'd blown the myth: eroding
tool marks and vertical planes gave it up as
a disused quarry, the yellow-stone lode for
the soot-black Broad Lane farms. But you
couldn't tell them; they chose to cleave to the
famous story: the German plane that missed
the pit and bombed the autumn cornfield.

They came from different earths, to work here in
the pits; slaved to shifts, slammed in
redbrick council estates, withered to work
and the miners' welfare, they walked the
weekend land as tourists, building meaning
from locally available materials: ignorance,
fancy, fact and experience, coalescing as
mythic consensus.

The sandstone hearths are fallen, the fireside voices
still. The filled-in quarry, a ridge in the
rapefield. Sons of colliers and long-dead
ploughmen, walking their meaningless
earth.

Reverend John Harnett Jennings

Odds are, he was a bastard of the very worst sort: a
youngest-son, silver-spoon, spoilt child of
Empire, wet-nursed and punkawallered
through Dulwich and Keble Colleges, then
steamered back to Palamcotta, the city of his
birth, a missionary clerk with twin shiny-
eyed ambitions: bettering sambo and
servanted ease.

Lady Julia gave him refuge from his vapour-fit
burn-out, worn down by the heathen of the
Tamil Nadoo; idolatrous Hindoos, fanatical
Mohammedans, and those monkeys in suit-
coats, the Indian National Congress, their
Anti-Christ dream of Poorna Swaraj. All
Saints at Hooton, a sinecure with a stipend:
Sunday service, weddings and funerals,
tiffin with Her Ladyship and the Primrose
League.

*At midnight there was a cry made. Behold, the
bridegroom cometh.* They buried you in the
overspill cemetery, by Lady Julia's bishop-
blessed lych-gate. Perhaps you designed
your who's-who gravestone, white marble
with hammered-lead lettering, marking you
apart from the lock-jawed gritstones
standing mute in crass West Riding earth.
That's where I found you, pale and fading,
on your exile's grave.

Peacocks calling from the croquet lawn, wallahs
fetching cake and manzanilla; home from
home. Reverend Jennings, forgive my maybe
slanderous fancy: odds are, you were a
decent man; a saint, a scholar, hale-cleric-
well-met. Whatever you were, now cold in
our clays – your life belongs to me.

The Field Church, Frickley

Its Black Death village six centuries erased, All
     Saints stands at the end of the track, framed
     watercolour-perfect in churchyard trees.

The barred-door padlocked, stained-glass caged;
     loose slates, torn flashings. Close-mown sod
     around the ashlar, the tottery gravefield
     otherwise run to seed; in need of sheep to
     crop the grasses, goats to strim the weeds.

Now and then I visit: Cooks and Sorbys, yeoman
     of this parish, and their betters, the Aldams
     and Anns; Danny Clarke, much-missed and
     greatly-grieved, flowers and devotions
     weekly renewed; Laura Speight, and Edward
     her son, *who served at the alter of this church*;
     John Dale, faithful servant, cenotaph
     dwarfing his master's stone; Thomas
     Depledge, murdered on the highway;
     generations of uncairned ploughmen, long-
     dissolved to feeding nitrates, richening our
     earth.

Mass said monthly, every second Sunday: Father
     Lethbridge, three white-haired ladies, a man
     with a well-behaved dog. And someone
     without, yearning for communion,
     prayerful, hymn-less, fumbling for words,
     carving his name on trees.

Monk Bretton Priory

Sharp left before the roundabout at Cundy Cross,
    straight on past the chippy and into the
    estate. Turn right into the red shale car park,
    and there it stands, the ruin of the Priory of
    Mary Magdalene of Lund, ringed in its
    precinct by the shedded back-gardens of
    council bungalows.

The signage is bent and over-scrawled – *Rachel luvs
    Scott* – and here a fag butt, there a drained
    bottle of Bud. But over the muted traffic-
    roar, familiar stillness, sprung sod and soft
    sandstone soaking up sound, roofless walls
    still claiming due reverence from the land.

Gatehouse standing squarely, floor plan plain;
    church and cloister, refectory, dorter, leats
    running down to the Dearne. The slit-
    windowed hall for worldly business; rents
    from the chartered market, fleece and
    mutton from the grange; Cluny's profit,
    prayer *in perpetua*, the praise of the relayed
    choir exorcising the ingrate silence that
    mocked the hours of the Office.

Circuiting the site, processing first impressions, inevitable comparisons with Byland, Rievaulx, Roche. Aesthetic disappointment; no tumbled towers in a sylvan dale, or gleam of milky limestone, but soot-stained sandstone, housing sprawl, warehouse roofs and willow-herb wasteland. Salvaged as afterthought: absentee coal-lords, the muck-'n'-brass brutalists of the planning committee and bread- and-circus miners' welfare, converging in neglect, agreeing on irrelevance.

Rise and fall: Lund Priory, the farms and granges, the pit top winding gear; even Stairfoot's Burger King. The day is for the quick and the dead are in their graves. Hewing and piling in separate earths, men labour at their monuments, nailed from the womb into coffins of bone. Nothing survives but the *laus perennis* of stone.

Roche Abbey

Cathedral hush in the padded valley: the ivory crag of Table Rock, muffled with foliage and crawling ivy, lowering from the north; Grange Wood opposite, darkening to the dike, ash-crowns swelling and breathing; dike in rumbling spate, the reredorter smell of loam and wild garlic drifting over mown lawns opening to the east, Capability's stunning vista: ruinous walls of lichened stone, monumental transepts stilling the silvery air.

Sancta Maria de Rupe, Holy Mary of the Rock, raised heavenward from earth-hewn stone in the time of red-haired Henry: Norman loot-Lords, de Bully and fitzTurgis, rinsing their sins in Benedict's bought absolution; patronage of land, an abbot and twelve holy brothers: necessary simony, accommodation with the fallen world.

An army of men must have swarmed in this valley for decades, realising the *opus dei*: stonecutters, carpenters, craftsmen in lead and metal, each laddering skyward on tottering scaffolds, hauling hemp-roped pulleys and cranes: to raise this refuge in jointed ashlar, in praise of God, the glory of nameless men.

Green woodpeckers probing the walls of the
cloister, snaking like wrynecks.
Membranous harebells, nodding from
infilled rubble. Dogs in the columned forest,
yelps ringing off Laughton Pond;
clambering kids in the goth-graffitoed
gatehouse, surrendered and dissolute – *opus
anglicanum*, fat Henry's vernacular
wrecking-ball: mobs from Firbeck, Levitt
and Stone, stripping lead, pinching paving
and quarrying walls, bringing down the very
thing they thought well of, that genius of the
race, that they might sport and profit from
the spoil.

Tom Depledge

Playing pitch-and-toss with gypsies, Tom Depledge
won a piebald mare; short-backed, round
withers, plenty of feather. He rode her
bareback through the ings, home to
Clayton-in the-Clay.

The ambush came at Houghton: John and Billy
Lodge, with blackthorn clubs, horseshoes in
a stocking.

Van Diemen buried the Lodge boys. Tom lies in the
yard of the Field Church at Frickley, where
Rich rang the bells and legged it, this year I
planted mistletoe.

A Lytle Gest of John Nevison

And walke vp to the Saylis,
And so to Watlingr Strete,
And wayte after some vnkuth gest,
Vp chaunce ye may them mete.

A Lytle Gest of Robyn Hode

John Nevison was a Yorkshire boy, born in Pomfret
town; he didn't like work, preferred to shirk,
and strut his stuff around.

Nevison was a highway thief, along the Great
North Road; he robbed the rich, man and
bitch, with flintlocks *à la mode*.

Nevison taxed the drovers, from Catterick to The
Smoke; for a fee, he'd guarantee, safe
passage for bint or bloke.

Nevison bunked at the Blue Bell Inn, by the bridge
there on the Went; where he supped shine
beer and fenced snide gear, cause the
landlady was bent.

Nevison was a wanted man, but he didn't give a
damn; quick on the draw, a stone outlaw,
living on the lam.

Nevison robbed the rich alright, but he gave nowt
to the poor; but that was OK, cause it made
their day, to see toffs get fleeced for sure.

Nevison mugged a nob one day, up at Barnsdale
Bar; he stole his horse, his gold of course,
then bade him *au revoir*.

Nevison roared through Saylis Wood, down to his
   Blue Bell den; the militia in wait, he jumped
   the gate, and raced for Thorpe Audlen.

Nevison lost the tracking hounds, in Wrangbrook's
   sucking mire; he went to ground, thief's-
   honour bound, with scum from all the Shire.

Nevison holed at Adam's inn, on Brierley's
   Ringstone Hill; the gold he cached, in his
   oak-tree stash, on the verge of old Ryknil.

Nevison paid young Adam well, but he paid Old
   Adam more; because you see, that was the
   tree, named thus in Brierley-lore.

Nevison boozed and bet and brawled, in Adam's
   den of vice; but he nailed his bride, by the
   dim fireside, while the groom was pitching
   dice.

Nevison knew the game was up, with the lead-shot
   through the door; he'd had his fun, now he
   had to run, over snitching Adam's whore.

Nevison vaulted from the sash onto his bare-back
   mare; naked in boots, and under-scoots, in
   the freezing winter air.

Nevison raced down Ryknil, militia in hot pursuit;
   musket-fire and finks for hire, hollering,
   'Where's the loot?'

Nevison slipped the hue-and-cry in the dungeon
   of Nor Wood; where he jumped a nark, and
   did remark, 'yon Adam has the goods'.

Nevison laughed-out-loud to see young Adam in
the dock; fined five pound, his sign took
down, for letting outlaws run amok.

Nevison slunk right back that night, to Old Adam's
trunk-stash hoard; and with great stealth,
retrieved his wealth, still safely in there
stored.

Nevison rode to the Magpie Inn, at Sandal by the
castle; win or lose, he was on the booze,
regardless of coppers' hassle.

John Nevison was a Ponty boy, and so, you toffs,
are we; so one-by-one, *bring it on* – in the
shadow of the gallows tree.

Invicta

On the summit of a mound of demolition rubble,
    looking west to a Wimpey's sunset; the
    Invicta Knitting Mill, its fifty year course full
    run. Red-brick turrets tumbled, lawned
    frontage run to fireweed waste. Our
    seventies not-so-secret garden, sky-lit
    rooftop playground: dead as textiles.

Memories, half-truths, possible fictions: daredevil
    Deano, falling from the flagpole tower;
    deathless feasts on laburnum pea-trees; pie-
    crust against the windowed walls, war
    games, spud fires, best-man-falls; our Pirate-
    proof castle on the rampart-roof, tooled to
    the teeth; half-charlies, claysticks, red diesel
    molotovs.

We were all there: Ness, Wack and Neck; Keithy,
    Julius, Georgie and Peebag; Cyril and
    Egghead, Albert Einstein, Linnit, Lippy and
    Curts: and so were they; PC Stacey,
    Councillor Brightman, Johnny Bradley and
    the Park Estate Pirates – but they couldn't
    get us down.

Spearhafoc

for Hines, Loach and Bradley

No cleric am I, yet a sperviter and a musketeer.
My quarry whatever the woods provide;
nuthatch, bullfinch, long-tailed tit,
deciduous ortolans. I calibrate by
candlelight in screamless plywood mews;
gauntlet, jesses, vitamin B12.

Sharp-set's frugal fare: gassed hatchlings, snap-
trapped mice; bowsed in watered blood.
Tight-fletched bow-perch, taut as catgut;
wasp-eyed, frantic, bristling with blades.

Sabbath-dawn in the yeomanned wood; no cleric,
and yet no knave; egg-thief, scrumper of
eyasses, plucker of pointless fowls; redstart,
blackcap, golden oriole.

Old Adam

The year of the hairy star: Tostig and Sigurdsson
   fell, Harald the English King; and an acorn
   in the royd on Ryknild, by the crossroads on
   the common.

There they stood, the Well-Bred Oaks, somehow
   surviving when the wildwood surrounding
   was cleared into common and open field.
   Tabooed by naval and ecclesial planksmen,
   escaping estover and creeping enclosure,
   over centuries swelling to girthy senescence;
   a stag-horned, hollow-heart, branch-
   dropping, pleistocene herd.

Somehow indeed: Ringstone's sacred grove, the old
   religion forgotten but reverence remaining?
   (Oak Royd was Feast Royd, the embanked
   arena of the Good Friday wake.) Pressed-
   militia drillfield, wapentake muster,
   beacon-hill with the thirty mile vista? Or
   something less definable – handed-down
   folk-awe: the gnarly guardians of the
   thousand-acre common?

Reasons regardless, the oaks endured, dying slowly
   over centuries until only two remained: the
   Adam and Eve Oaks, site of new moon rites
   for childless women; and then, by
   Cromwell's time perhaps, just one: Old
   Adam, trunk stash for Nevison's loot,
   landmark for travellers, tourist attraction in
   Hunter's *South Yorkshire*.

Three Victorian gentlemen, posing in front of a
    misnomered tree – 'the Elliott oak at the
    Wind Gap, Brierley': mutton-chop whiskers,
    jaunty-casual poses, Bill Sykes played by
    Oliver Reed. Half the tree has fallen away,
    the beginning of the end; water-rot, honey
    fungus – a hump of sheep-cropped sod.

In decades, the bounded royd ploughed-out, the
    common annexed into tonne-turning
    hectares. And lately the last, lingering
    connection, the Good Friday feast – snuffed
    out like the paschal candle, the communion
    finally broken. Doomed survivor of an
    extinct congregation, I make my stand on
    Ringstone, vigil for a flame that can never be
    rekindled.

Winter nightwalk

Blanketing snow has smothered the night in hush. Traffic roar absent, cars drifted to their street-lit kerbs. Owls puffed up in hawthorns, foxes quivering in holes; just me on the path from Ringstone Hill, my boot-steps in the creaking snow, the only sound in the Universe.

Snow at night creates its own light, a soft luminosity, dulling the world in glow; in which the footpath stretches before me, a blue slash through the winter-wheatfield, moon-illumined to the chopped horizon and the edge of Howell Wood. I halt at the stile where the trees begin, in the silence of the snow.

Bluebells lie dormant in the peaty loam, as they have at this time since the melting of the glaciers, before stone axes sounded in the forest and hand-ploughs opened the sod. Perhaps it was these, our neolithic fathers, who ringed hengestones on the hill, long smashed into wall-stone by puritan sledgehammers? Only the name and mystery remain.

Clumped flakes are falling, bouffant and mute, effacing this time, but not place; and with the world buffered out, the spirits come jostling: Anglian farmers hauling home harvest, breaking bread in the beery oxgang; salt-burned Norse, glistening with pig-meat, feasting from east and west hagues; gleaners bearing baskets on balks and byways, cottars picking sticks in the gorsey assart; vardos circled on the wood-smoke common, colliers in mufflers, ploughmen harrowing tilth: generations have trod these humdrum acres, lives written and erased in the palimpsest of earth; but in the snow-stilled quiet of a winter's night, in mind, in fancy, or on the plasm direct, you can hear the cacophonous landscape calling: a fair field full of folk in clamorous reunion, saluting the mongrel blood that runs in the veins of kindred men.

Big Billy

Listen! Lament for Laddie, the lauded long-dog,
hammer of hares, harrow of foxes,
killer of coneys, curse of field-flushed cats.
Leash-slipped, spuming, slaughterlust blinded,
slavver-tongue tight to a turning hare,
he blood-crazed crashed through cruciate wire
first-light this fair feast-Friday morning.
Gullet-gashed, gralloched, gutsnakes gleeting,
ligged lacerate limp in the hoar-frost ley,
catgut-crochet, the courser's catholicon,
would wire no more the whimpering war-dog whole.
Big Billy built his backyard barrow
and spade-back tamped the turf down tight.
The shire-shouldered soil-shifter stood
and swaled the sweat from his swarth and said:
he were a bloody good dog.

Brusson Big Billy, beat-em-all brawler,
bane of bullies and blathering blowhards,
best of Barnsley, bar-blessed Ponty's pride.
Pit-man, poacher, pint-pot playboy,
feast-bound, fired-up, famous for the fight.
Word wound its way to his mam's house;
Welsh-windbag, Whalehead Jones,
pit-top blacksmith and beerhall bouncer,
had chelped out a challenge; he'd champ any man
on the Test-Your-Strength, Tyrone Tucker's
storied Striker, its thirty-foot summit bell
in fifty feasts unrung. 'The fat-fart's full of it,'
Billy said, 'I'll ring that bell, and batter off a peal
from his bucket-bonce as well.'
                                    The busful to Brierley
piled-out palavering, plastered and pluckful,
pledging to pleasure; but Billy and his boys
strode straight to the Striker, rolling their shoulders
and darting dead-eyes. Ty drummed them up;
'Are there Mighty Men here, or just Mammy's Boys?'
Mumbles, murmurs, then the massed crowd parted,

potgut Whalehead whelming through; a bear-whelped
ape-armed, beetle-browed brute,
muscle-masher, mangler, maimer of men.
'Who here is willing to whack with Jones?
A pound for a pound, I'll puck-pummel higher
and make any geezer that gainsays a liar.'
The lads lurched forward, lusting to prove
their hammer-hefting strength, but Billy bid them halt:
'We'll watch a while this windy chuff,
the chaps that chance it; then I'll champ this chump.'
A bloke broke ranks, brazened to the booth,
and pressed a pound in Whalehead's palm;
'I'll pick your pocket, pumpkin-pate.'
No-Neck Barratt, Brierley bruiser,
gouger, grappler, pit-prop-forward
beefed and butty, squat as a bollard.
The hard-eyed hoof-handler hurled him the hammer
and sneered for him to start. Spit-gripped,
wrist-strapped, the stumpy scrummager
smashed the down the mallet; the puck shot-skyward;
not *Weed*, nor *Reckling, Mammy's Boy* or *Mister*,
the powered-puck peaked at twenty-five foot,
a height hardly reached by he-man or hero.
The crowd-crowed and cast their caps aloft,
cheering the challenger, chanting his title:
'*Strongman! Strongman!*' The thug-smug Welsher
strutted to the Striker and lip-curl snickering,
stripped to his fat-swaddled waist. '*Strongman* my arse.
I'll best this beery butterball, first banging the gavel
and then *his* Halloween head.' Hale Whalehead,
hammer-humping horse-hitter, hefted the haft
and swung the sledge-head hard to the smack-pad,
sending the sore puck soaring: twenty seven foot!
Hail hammering Whalehead! – *Hercules*!
The bar-bending iron-smith bellowed his triumph
and roared rampaging round the ring
as the crowd cringed and cowered.
Beaten Barratt offered his humbled hand.

'Well-won Welshman. We whacked,
the best man won. Must we now welter?'
Whalehead waddled to noble No-Neck
and grinning, gripped his gracious hand.
'*Pumpkin-pate*, pissant? A pound
and a pounding, a pagan pagga,
your punch-up, punk-fit pay.'
The ball-bellied boor booted Barratt
in the ballocks and headbutt-broke his nose.
The wolfish Welshman worked him over,
stamping and raking the prone-prop still.
The hushed-horde parted; No-Neck's ruck-mates
barrowed him bashed away. Whalehead bayed:
'Bring the bastards on! Which boyo has the balls
to juke with Jones?' He prowled the pressed arena,
thundering and thrusting, thumping his chest,
threatening to thrash any thrall who'd step up.
Lips bit bloody, Big Billy buried his itching fists
deep in his Donegal pockets. 'Don't bite boys!
Now is not my time. See, another knuckler's
backing his brawn against this bonehead berk.'
Once more the mauling mob gave ground,
and swaggering swathed through Ambrose Samson,
the barbell-bouncing press-up prince,
shirtless, skin-shaved, corded with muscle.
Fearless Ambrose faced the fist-fiend
and stared down into his sheep-shit eyes.
'A pound for a pillock, a pillock for a pound.
I'll pan that pad and prang the bell,
then serve you the same and send you to hell.'
The stone-skulled savage stilled his storm
and blank-eyed, bowed off blandly smirking:
'Then the peopled floor is yours; pan away, pretty boy.'
Samson strode to the pine-stocked swing-bat
and flipping and flaunting, flashed the hammer
hand-to-hand. Hatching harm,
he grasped the gavel with gravel-grained grip
and bull-roar banged the batterer down.

The blurred puck pelted, greased in its groove;
gawpers-gasped and hat-hurled; *eight* and twenty foot!
A new *Hercules*, humbling the hated old!
Samson preened and paraded his pecs;
gaffers gawked, girls goggled and giggled.
'That's the first-fruits, fatty. Fair play, though,
take your thwack; then I'll thump you flat on your back.'
Whalehead wheezed and waddled to the whomp-plate.
Chuntering curses, he chalked his grip
and neck-silk strapped the slam-stock tight.
The ham-hocked hellion hoisted the hammer
and planet-plunged the brunt-edged peen,
poshing the pad, the puck up-plummeting,
blemming to the bell and barely falling short:
nine and twenty foot! Samson slack-jawed,
stumbled back, but the bone-breaking blackguard,
frantic with fury and fearing a fistfight,
flailed the flange-head flush to his forehead,
dropping him deadweight, grogged on the grass.
The crowd cringed and caught its breath;
girls screamed forward, succouring Samson,
cradling their buff-boy's busted bonce.
Whalehead trash-talked, taunting his triumph:
'Boo-hoo, babes, your bum-boy's battered;
dump the dickless-dork in the ditch.
I'm your *Hercules*, he-man, hero
the fellow to fettle faggot – or bitch.
Who now will knuckle with knock 'em dead Jones?'
All eyes turned to the tap-room terror,
cosher of cozzers, cobblestone king:
Big Billy, bull-built, battle-hard bruiser,
strode to the scratch-mark and scanting fear,
bellied up to the barbarous bear-whelp.
'I'll master you, monster. I'll man you
with the mallet, then maul you in the mud.
False-heart fouler,your flim-flam's finished.'
The blackhearted hammer-head curled his lip
and slimed a grass-snake sneer.

'A big boy brave in beer. But bottled-up battlers
are bound to bite off more than they can chew.
Chat is cheap, chuck-out-time Charley,
so gird your guts and grab the gavel: let's go.'
The brutal boor-banger battled back
blood-rage and handed-back the hammer:
'*You* set the standard, slanderous slugger;
I'll slam shortly and surely smash your mark.'
Stone-dome shrugged and spat.
'No matter, fool; first or last, I'll feat you
fair or foul.' He shouldered the sledge-head
and swanked to the Striker, glaring and goading,
hackling the hustings to hissing hate.
His hulking horse-handlers slathered in chalk,
hammer frapped firm to his freighted-forearms,
the wall-browed walloper strode-out a run-up,
a madman's momentum to master the mauler,
a desperate design to defeat the dauntless decklord.
Whalehead paced and pawed his soil-scratch
raging himself to hang-dog hate,
then hollering, hurtled hard to the hoickpad
and hammered the hulking hurlbat down.
The spanked puck spouted and summited in its slot;
twenty-*eight*, twenty-*nine* – the tiniest ting – *thirty* foot:
not humble *Hercules*, but *Mighty Thor!*
Jackhammer-Jones, Welsh-Wonder,
blueblood basher of beetles, ringer of the virgin bell!
Wild-eyed Whalehead crashed the cordon
and howled around the Waltzer, whirling wenches,
bowling blokes aside. Vainglorious in victory,
he knee-slid screaming into Billy's face:
'Beat that big-shot; give best
to broad-backed Jones, the bell-blasting King
of the fifty year feast.' The fearless fist-fiend
stepped past him to the Striker. 'Savour your boasting,
brag-bloated clown; with this blow
I'm taking you down.' The unmastered-maimer
seized the sledge-stock and sauntered the edge

of the toiling throng, twirling the troll-tamer
effortless over his head. 'Enough of this egg-head's
piss-poor posturing, his panoply of pap;
Beetle-first, I'll better the boor
then fist the flatulent fraud to the floor."
The downer of doormen danced to the Striker
and heel-screwed deep his soil-set stance.
Hobnail-anchored, he swung the steelhead,
loosening sinews and shift-stiff shoulders.
Then, supple and sanguined, surging with sway,
the anvil-armed Antaeus hoisted the hammer
and smashed down the sky-swung smiter.
The peen-panned puck pelted to the pinnacle
and wrecked the rocket-rang bell –
hammerlord, metal-masher, even *Mightier Thor*!
The crowd surged and swarmed the thump-thegn,
a flurry of flat-caps, hand-shakes and back-slaps,
the champion cheer-chaired over the feast-field.
Beer-tent tankards tipped and drained
and Spion Kop battle-hymns bawled:
'Big Billy! There's only one Big Billy!"
But a varicose voice vexed the arena:
'Churls, cease cheering. This challenge is not over.
A fist-fight finals, finishing doubt
whether welting Jones or this wideboy wanker
is the common-crowned King of Clout.'
The lauded lamp-lord leapt to earth
and rolled right up to the roughhouse ring.
Belly to belly with the bested blacksmith,
the fearsome feast-fiend offered his fair-play hand:
'Bravo, braggart with balls of brass;
well-beaten you banter to battle Big Billy.
Maybe a man-heart mallets within after all.
Beyond doubt you are a blustering bully-boy,
but now, it seems, no craven coward.
Now knuckle-up, knurl, and ready for the knock-out.'
Feet-set, fists-raised, faced-up for the fight,
the trusting termagant reined in his rampage

and held back from hitting as Whalehead girded,
readying to roister; then, without warning,
the shameful-shamster whipped from his waistband
a strop-sharped shiv and snaking forward, slashed.
Billy bucked and bounced away, blood-bubbling
from his bicep, blade-bit to the bone.
The slinker circled, seeking to stab
the chopped-arm churl-champ,
now roused to rage like a baited-bear:
'No man, nor monster, but a mange-marred dog
that bites the hand that feeds; fat-fool,
press together your palms and pray;
provoked, I'll pummel and pulverise,
man-mangle, massacre, muller you in the mud.'
The pub-praised pounder prowled and closed,
cornering the cozener, cutting off his flight.
Daunted and desperate, the doomed Welshman
once more darted out the dagger, deepening his shame.
Set for the switchblade, the sure-footed man-bane
swayed back and slipped the lunge-slash,
and seeing the gap in the growling-grouthead's guard:
falcon-fast, the fearless finisher of men
hooked a howitzer over the knife-arm
into the hellbound-hitman's head.
The sound of splintering skull-plates
cracked across the crowd; sockets shattered,
cheek and jaw bones broke: the burly-batterer
dropped to the dirt like a pole-axed-bull,
flat-backed, blood-blathered, slaughter-block still.
Shocked to silence, the slack-jawed frape
fringed-forward to gawp at fist-frushed Jones,
a broken bloodsack, barely breathing
mangled to bone-crocked, moaning meat.
Big Billy, man-masher, merciless mauler,
straddled the field-flopped fist-fraud
and trumpeted his triumph. 'This ten-men
tough will trade his terror no more.
Give best to Big Billy, bane of big shots,

feted fettler of the feated feast-field!'
The fight-flushed rabble roared their approval
and nobbings rained down for the noble knuckler.
Ty's boy brought a bucket, brimful from the spring:
sponge-swabbed, slash-stitched
collared and cologned, the cobblestone-clobberer,
pockets packed with coined applause,
brought the boys to the brawling beerhall
to hoist and holler, get hammered.

> Stewards stretchered the slam-sick Welshman
> to the waiting wagon. Waist-stripped,
> drivelling and dislocate, the dent-head demon
> lurched and lolled in St. John's cradling canvas,
> seeping-scarlet, spittering teeth.
> Blown with broom, the four-manned bier
> crawled through crowds to the cart-clogged crossroads.
> Wreathed in whin, garlanded in gorse,
> the humbled humbug hauled into the ambulance,
> which, siren wailing, whisked him away,
> to Warde Aldam on Westfield Lane.
> Breeze-bashed blackthorns blizzarded blossom
> across the fight-field's flattened arena.
> Soiled and spoiled on stamped-sward strewn,
> Whalehead's scarf, his collarless-shirt,
> blazer and billycock hat – boys brazening
> to pillage and pick the pockets,
> showmen shouting the shameless thieves away.

Pint-pots, pillocking, party-time;
lads laughing and lathered,
lurching and leering at booze-loosened lasses.
Flesh-flashing, flirty, the fresh-faced fillies
bar-barged Billy, bantering for beer,
pouting promises for paid-on porter.
The lion-loined leatherer lined up the glasses
and bade the bints and boys imbibe:
'Sisters, sidekicks: salute Sam Smiths!

Sod-sobriety! Sluts and slicks, get smashed!'
The tanked-up tipplers tilted their tumblers
and toasted the tent-taverned troll-trasher,
as rumour rippled through the roister
and battened at the bar. Beer-bleared,
Billy woke to the word, a wager whizzed
from the boxing booth, barrelhead-cash,
winner-take-all: will the whomper of Whalehead
risk his rep and rumble with Mankiller Sykes,
pro-pugilist, pummeller, fair-field punch-out king?
At stake, a score, if the scrape-sore scuffler's
standing still after three sledgehammering rounds.
The half-cut hard-man bottomed his beer
and bounded for the booth. 'Bladdered or not
I'll back my brawl against this ballyhooed bum.
Lads, lend your lucre; let's lay it on these fists;
In nine gloved minutes, I'll guarantee
to double our dough; I'll dump this dosser,
then royally-ratted we'll riot and roister
next work-wagged week away.'

Lenny Sykes, Lupset Legend,
the heavyweight hitter that hammered Bill Hague;
Big Jack Beckett's bang-out bane,
the brute that bested Bombardier Billy.
Slammed in Strangeways for slotting a copper,
he knuckled a nark and nailed him dead,
gaining his murderous moniker: Mankiller Sykes,
most feared and formidable fighting man
never to land the Lonsdale Belt.
Bare to his breeches, Billy bandaged his hands
and stared at his savage-set foe:
beer-bellied, balding, his best days over,
yet bristling like a battle-worn bear:
the slugger who sparred sixty rounds with Jack Johnson,
him canvas-crashing and counting out
with a jolting jab to the jaw.
Glimpsing his gaze, the grizzled-grappler

stood from his stool and snarled across the ring:
'Peep on, you punch-drunk pipsqueak:
Sykes has gone soft, I see you thinking,
a globe-gutted grey-beard, a geezer gone to seed.
Well, in these gloves I guarantee, are guns to gimp,
lay-out and litter, a likely lad like thee.'
The hale-hearted hot-head strode to scratch
and gave him glare for glare: 'Give it up,
you gormless gorilla. Great you were once,
respected ringside round the world
and doubtless deadly to drunken farmboys still.
But I've banged-out bullies from Blackpool to Brid;
trust me, I'm taking your twenty quid.'
The crowd crushed to the canvas,
baying their bets; the booth-boss bade
both brawlers to their corners, then binged
the first round bell; let battle begin!
Whalehead's waster walled up his gloves
and circled the senile slayer of men,
pawing and probing, priming for the punch.
The monstered mauler moved slowly to cover,
rolling, retreating, rocking on the ropes –
then feinting, fired a fearsome fist
that detonated like dynamite, denting Billy's skull.
Stars surged and shattered in swimming blackness
and as strength sapped from his spasming legs,
the fearless feaguer floor-bound flopped.
Gloves aloft, the gloating gamecock
crowed to his corner, as Billy crawled
on canvas, climbing ropes to beat the count.
Gawpers gasped and gamblers groaned,
but the teak-tough terror tottered aloft on nine.
Blear-brained, blurry, the battered brawler
coiled and covered as the club-king kill-closed,
hooking and hammering, each hulking blow
landing like a lumphead, lifting and lurching
the plucky pitman, pounding him hard to the prayed-for-bell.
Slack-jawed, stool-sat, slapped to his senses

by smelling salts and slathering sponge,
the fist-fazed feast-fiend blinked himself clear.
'This gnarly knuckler's knacking me good,
hitting as hard as the heft of a horse.
I'll spoil to survive, and crowd in close,
constricting the space he needs to swing free.'
Round two, Billy, clutching and crowding,
clinched the cursing clubber in corners,
but the bestial bruiser banged kidneys
and ribcage, each corpse-crunching impact
smashing and splatting like meat under steel.
Three mauling minutes had almost passed
when the punch-crazed punisher prised himself free
and pistoned a piledriver that pummelled so hard
it gashed glove and gushed gore
from the gape it gouged in Billy's grim face.
The round-end ringer rattled its knell
and the maestro of malice mugged-off the crowd
gloves-raised, gleeful, glowering down.
Meanwhile, stool-set, coursing claret,
the chastened champion called
for a clamp to crimp the blood flow
from his clout-carved cheek. Sykes capered ringside,
still signalling success, but his split-glove
spilled its shameful secret: a shire-shoe
gripped within the glove, giving the Mankiller
his awesome punching power. Stunned punters
hushed the roped-arena, as roused to rage,
the righteous roughneck raised erect.
'Sykes, you scheming scumbag!
Your punching prowess is a perfidious scam,
your fake-fame framed on fraudulent fists.
Though bruised and battered from your base betrayal,
I'll serve you savage and show you true
Big Billy's no man to mess with:
a mastiff-mean-mullerer, a mauler of men,
a champ of chumps and chuntering cheats like you.'
Sneering Sykes stripped off his bloodsmeared mitts,
and slammed *two* shire-shoes down. 'So I swindled

a swanker, swelled with self-regard; so what?
To win's the thing, to walk wadded
from the ring. Rip off those rabbit-punchers
and mittless meet me like a man; all in.'
Blood boiled in Billy's barbarian brain
and tunnelled his vision in sanguined blur;
roaring he raced across the rope-ring
and bare-fist banged the black-heart blaggard
on the cleft of his crag-hard chin.
Knuckle and jaw-bone broke; the bully-boy
slumped and starfished-flat, spark-out on the boards.
Candescent with rage, the carnage-crazed champion
straddled Sykes' sack-slumped carcass
swinging mug-mashing fist-shots left and right,
splintering sockets and champing cheekbones
until stewards and samaritans swarmed the ring
and dragged the demented destroyer away.

Calmed-down, cloth-cleaned, stitched back together,
the crocked king of carnival cradled his ale
in broken hands, bruised and bloated to blackening stubs.
Raw-ribbed, face-ripped, addled with aching,
the war-sore Woden whetted his whistle,
each poured pint dulling the pain.
And the lathered lads lifted their glasses and lauded:
'Big Billy! You'll never beat Big Billy!'

Death's-door damaged, dumped broken
on blood-slicked boards, the brutalised bully-boy
hauled himself upright and, hardy of heart,
hobbled to hole-up in his healing van.
For three dire days and desperate nights,
single-malt medicine paralyzed the pain,
until the soused avenger sawed off a shotgun
and stumbled out to settle his score.
Shooter sheathed beneath his suit-coat,
the stricken slugger searched the streets, seeking satisfaction
in a both-barrelled blast that'd serve bold Billy true.
But pig-bled, pummelled and whisky-weak

his pump packed-in at Elmsall's Plough,
where the game old grappler gave up the ghost
supping Sam's in the saloon bar.
They gouged his grave at George's church:
his mother mourned, the minister mouthed the service.

Beer-balmed, blarneyed, blissfully blotto,
Big Billy, the brawl-battered battler,
counted his combat-claimed coin.
Leisure looked likely, a week-long laiker;
ligged in bed, bollixed in the boozer,
Brid or Blackpool bound.
But a burly brigand barged through the bar-crowd
and backed by bruisers, banged a fat wad down.
Correr Mush, King of the Gypsies
bare-fist best of the travelling breeds,
had come to call-out the crust-crushing clobberer.
'Gorger, get your greenbacks down.
A ton says we'll tussle, tear-up on the turf.
A death-matched didacoi, undefeated,
I wager I'll win and wallet the wonga;
Match me, mauler, meet me man-on-man.'
The boys bounced up: 'Back-off, beggarman,
the knuckler's knackered, his nut knotted,
his mitts mashed and massacred.
Two mighty men he's mullered this day,
in wearying-wars that wore him down
and surely-sapped his strength;
a month to mend, he'll man you, Mush,
but now he's in no slug-fit state:
so push-off, pikey, our pal's played-out
and presently pledged to peace.'
Correr's cronies crowded in
and belly to belly the bellicose boys
faced-off. The fair-field fettler
stood from his stool and stayed the stand-off:
'Correr, cool your half-cocked hot-heads down.
The bout's between yourself and Billy;

let's leave our lads well-out.
And though my body's black and blue,
my muscle-meat malleted tender,
for a hundred pounds I'll haul my hide
to whatever rough-ring you ryes require.
My hurt hands may haymakers hinder
and hold me back from havocking hits,
but even busted, boy, I'll best you,
girding guts and guile and mettle
to master, in lieu of mangling mitts.'
The Romany ruffian reached-out and squeezed
the hard-bit heath-fiend's held-out hand.
'Well-said, warrior. We'll welter yon,
beyond the wagons, on the way-cross waste.
There, no doubt I'll double my dosh,
for, despite your devil, I discern my grip
pangs pain, provoking you to wince.'
The renowned ruffians rolled to the rough-field,
swarmed by steaming, scrap-crazed crowds.
The boys begged Billy reconsider,
but the strife-scarred scuffler shook his head.
'Fracas-frayed or fighting-fresh,
a melee for money's my meat and drink;
besides, once challenged, a champ must chance it;
the bloke backing down is a bottling blackguard,
a no-mark nancy, not fit for praise nor fame.
This tinker's a terror to traveller and collier,
a rogue to be reckoned with, respect-worthy rye.
But the bloke's not born can beat Big Billy,
so wind-up your wittling – and watch me
whack this warlike warg sky-high'

Fists-bound, bating, the bare-chest battlers
shuffled and shadow-boxed, swaggering to the scratch-mark.
Holding the hot-headed hellions apart,
the ref ran through the prize-ring rules,
and knuckles knocked, the noble Nimrods
waded in, and walloping, went to war.

Mush malleted-madly, a maelstrom of punches;
combinations clashed and clattered,
hooks and headshots, hammering jabs.
Billy baulked each broadside with battening biceps,
and each fistic-fusillade forearm foiled,
before banging the bruiser back to the crowd-wall
with jolting jabs and jaw-jarring crosses.
Blooded, the brave boys backed and circled,
each eying the enemy, searching
for a stratagem to settle his foe.
But Billy's bandaged, bone-broke hands
fluid-filled and fluxed with blood,
were gnarled and nerve-numb, in need of nursing;
each shot he slammed sent shards
of shock-pain surging through his skull.
Billy's best blows had barely bruised
the green-lane grappler, who gloated in glee
to his gore-greedy breed. 'Game is this gorger,
but gammy of glove; his licks land like a little-lass's.
Frittered on feast-fame, his fight has faltered,
leaving the lauds and the lucre to me.
I'll fly in fiercely and fire this fake spark-out.'
Frail of fist, his hammers harmless,
the nail-hard hit-man held up his hands
in hollow hostility. 'Hold on to your hubris, pikey.
Haggard though my hands may be, I'm hale of heart
and hard of head, and though half-hobbled,
standing; scrap-scrounger, heed my words:
punchless perhaps, but fighting proud,
my will to war-wage waxes cruel.
Reckon the rules, and rule them out:
my advantage is all-in.'
Brave-words, but Billy's strength was seeping,
reflex wrecked and ringcraft raw;
seizing the moment, Mush made his move
and flew across the fight-floor, feinting a left
before ramming a right hook hard to the head;
Billy buckled under the blow and dropped to one knee,

brain-blurred, blighted, battered half-blind.
Cruel Correr, cold-hearted cobble King,
closed in and clouted the half-collapsed collier,
punching him prone on the pagan field.
The mob roared and rolled forward;
the brutal breed backed-off;
Big Billy, the broken braveheart,
hauled to his haunches and sucked down air.
Snorting-snot and clots of claret,
he stumbled to scratch and raised his shattered fists.
'Mush, you midget. A man half-mullered
and you fail to finish? For shame.
Your fight is fake and your fame is fraud.
You've beat bugger-all but blustering pikeys,
backed by the bully-boys of your bandit breed;
valourless-vagrant, vile vardo-vagabond: step forward!
March to the mark and meet once more your master.'
Fire flashed from the fearless gypsy's eyes.
'No big-mouth miner will ever master Mush;
And, cursed-collier, for your calumnies – I'll kill you.'
The rage-filled rye raced roaring to the scratchmark,
smacking steel-hard slam-shots left and right.
Once more his mauling mitts connected,
and the wounded warrior warped to earth once more.
Blood-blind, broken, brain-lights blinking,
the slog-sore soldier struggled on in darkness
and flailed to feel the fight.
The death-matched didacoi dropped to earth
and grappled with the grounded great-heart,
pummelling, pounding, peppering punches,
frenzied for the finish. The fading fight-fiend,
battling blackness, groped blindly for his foe,
forcing fingers in eyeholes,
tearing at testicles, chawing off ears,
desperate savage, a snare-snagged wolf.
Mangled in mud, the martial marrers
mauled for mastery as the brawling mob rolled in,
to lambast the loser, laud their laurel-crowned King –

then, scrambling, screaming, streaming scarlet
the prince of pikeys panicked from the fray,
plucked-eyes string-swinging on scarlet cheeks.
The crowd sucked back, sickened to slack-jawed silence.
The gore-glazed gamecock gozzed out gristle
and clambered to his feet. Caked in clay,
basted in bloods, he bayed at the blinded bruiser,
gibbering in his gouged-out grime.
'Correr, you cur. You saw me crocked
and came to conquer, crippled though I am.
My strength was spent, my slug-fists broken,
my body, bashed and bled and bruised.
Yet I made it to the mark and more than matched you,
punishing your pride, chastising your cowardice,
finishing your fakery fair and square.
Three men this day have dared to duel
with Billy; each bloke I broke and banished.
Romany rye, ripped of eye and royally routed,
remember the rawp of this righteous throng.'
The lads loped over and beer-tent bound
dragged him arm-draped through the bellowing crowd:
'Big Billy! You'll never beat Big Billy!'

> The service, St Joseph's; Spurs and Leicester,
> Cup Final Day. His sons cornered the coffin
> in and out of church, to the committal in the clays
> of the Catholic cemetery. Women wept,
> blokes bowed their brylcreemed heads.
> A good turn-out, a lot of lads laiking,
> looking to get lathered later on in his name.
> The priest prattled him off to purgatory,
> parsimonious with praise; pitman, husband, father.
> He'd sickened since Christmas, shrunk
> to a shadow of his former self, savaged by disease:
> bronchitis, black-lung, some bane in the bone,
> blighted by brawling, Bensons and bitter.
> Sixty-one years old. Sandwiches at the Social,
> battenburg, buns and Brooke Bond tea.

Friends and family, formica-flocked,
growing from grief to relief.
Ties loosening, laughter, low voices
larking loud; a load beginning to lift.
Big Billy – bloody hell! A big-hitter
the like of we'll never lay eyes on again.
Do you remember –

The Harrowing of the North

*Then the King was informed that the men
of the North were gathered together and meant
to make a stand against him.*

Florence of Worcester,
(D) Chronicle.

Moorthorpe to Sheffield, 1983

Torp, the farmstead in the assart sloping
down to Ermsale; Edwin's manor, of Godwinson
King, where Swein and Archil held carucates
for geld; now a halt on the Leeds
to Sheffield line: cemetery, terrace-rows,
boarded-up shops.
              The seven-fifteen pulls away
to langthwaite, the Danelaw's wildwood clearing;
past the slacky grime of the coalman's yard,
the ramshack sawmill, the fumes of the dayglo
chemical works; the dog food factory's
blowfly drone, White City's blown washlines
and drab net curtains; the triple barbed-wire
of the cullet plant, the dumped settees
of the Broadway cutting – to the sprawling wolds
of Frickley tips. Fricca's lea, meadow of the Northman,
carved from bear-prowled Barnsdale when Alfred
was King, torn from England by the Bastard,
and sublet to absentee minions:
de Mortain, de Surdeval, Anns
and Warde-Aldams, planters of the pit,
policers of the people, privateers of plough.
Through Frickley's keepered, keep-out coverts,
the train rattles south through the arable to Thurnscoe,
Ternusc on ancient Ryknild. Slate-roof terraces,
coal-car sidings and the towering spoil
of Hickleton Main, crawling with Euclids
and bleeping dump trucks, truants backied-up
on pedal pop plaggys, opening the throttle
and scrambling away, from pit cops, rail cops
and the EWO.
              Stones smack off the window glass
and the train departs for Bolton, past the Highgate
flappers' track and the flat-faced diesel loco
curving the spur from Goldthorpe pit,

its thirty-two truck, eight hundred tonne load
headed for Thorpe Marsh, Ferrybridge, Drax;
past lofted backyards and the Welfare Ground
to the dead-end, back-road station,
jungled in willowherb and rickety elders,
framed by the destitute warehouse; windows broken,
hanging doors, 'LUFC rule', its crumbling apron
of broken concrete littered with crabs,
dropped from the feral platform tree. Bodeltone-
on-Dearne, Bolton-by-the-river, in the mere
and the ingas and the crane-clamoured kjarr.
Here, amid the reedmace and sedges
of the saturated coalfield shales, foundered
Olaf's Dublin Norse, fleeing from Brunanburh;
where Paganel usurper launched
haut vol peregrines at gleads and hernshaws,
and where the sucking slurries of Pierrepont's
Manvers Main stretch miles along the valley,
an offworld dystopia of nightlit
washeries and winding gear, lighting towers
and marshalling yards, slag heaps and sewage works,
smithies and workshops, heavy plant
and heavy metals, hectares of festering scrap;
concealed from Thoresby's Tory vistas
by a county's breadth, by Eton, Oxford
and the Rufford foxhounds.
                                        Avert your eyes
as the train moves south to Masborough,
past the Aldwarke bar and rolling mills,
coke heaps, freight cars and belching furnaces,
horizons of girders and rusting plate,
before squealing to a stop by Wrodger's
derelict chainworks, the rotted brickwork's
soot-veneer tigered by rainlash, groundsel
rooting in the mortar, trumpeting down
the walls. On, into the smoke-black tunnel,
carbon stalagtites rooting from the brickwork,
cables, switches and enveloping darkness,

blaring to light of silver graffiti,
bankrupt cutlers, engineering gone to the wall.
And the station itself, walled-in by bloodbrick
Millmoor, Booth's ferric Serengeti,
scrap cars and rusted metal lowering all
horizons.
        On towards Brightside, past sewage farm,
cooling towers and double-decked M1
to the fallen towers of Tinsley Steel, toppled
under blows from McGregor's crane-swung
wrecking balls. Across the valley to the south,
on the heath where Æthelstan humbled
the hoary traitor, throb the smoking halls
of Phoenix, Steel Peech & Tozer, hard-by
the stranded, council-estate chantry
in Egil's butterfly wood.
                Onward
to Attercliffe, Dresden-derelict,
a crushed brick wasteland where buddleia
and willowherb blow. Cyclops, Aetna and Vulcan
no more, the drop-hammers silenced
and coke ovens grey; Vickers and Cammel,
Lonhro's East Hecla, given up to the wreckers
and salvage yard, their bankrupt capital
fled to The City, to Jersey and to Man.
But here and there amid the rubble,
a remnant remains; scrapyards and tool shops,
specialist engineers; and men on hard corners,
shaking heads and pointing, to where something
used to be. Others, up with the reborn
day-shift larks, old habits dying hard,
taking early morning dog-walks
along building-less streets, for the paper,
perhaps, or something to do: swallowed
into the long dark gullet, of the tunnel
to Sheffield Midland: where I get out,
and the track flows south to London.

Battle

On the dark ridge
breaking above the sea fret
fourteen thousand
in mail and helmets
notched shields
and bloodrust axes
bristling with spears
like a smoking fen
the long roar
rising from the valley
barrel-chests
of rutting deer.

Dinnertime
in the Asda car-park
chilled pasties and Vimto
then a walk down the hill
to the trampled wheatfield
five thousand coppers in riot gear
visored helmets
squinting shields
and dangling batons
we take off our shirts
to catch some rays
and wait.

The shield wall held
against man-smashing
battery of horse
sky-darkening salvoes
flung javelins
the amputating sword
hatchet hacked
and blade-edge bit
three times his mounts
were cut beneath him
Gyrth and Leofwine
fell.

The word goes round
we move to the shield-wall
pressure mounts
the crush and shove begins
batons slam down
split skulls
stones from five mile snipers
tumble from the sun
the gate opens
and sixty revving lorries
swerve out and away
towards the shimmering M1.

Across the sucking blood-mire
quarterless battle raged
broadswords clashing
and sparking
splintering shields
until fletched ash pierced
the anointed orbit
and the kingless fled
their slain abandoned
for spoil of wolves
the buckle-billed ravens
of the Weald.

The shield-wall opens
stampeding horses
and snatch squads ride
shirtless in jeans and trainers
the lads pile in and scatter
Stivvy decks a cop
and Jonah's got a helmet
but Francey's clubbed
to intensive care
and Big Jeff's not moving
we flee to the railway
over the crimson wheatfield.

William the Bastard

William was the bastard son
of Robert of Normandy
and stinking Fulbert's daughter
from the Falaise tannery.

But don't despise the nameless boy
he was Robert's only son
and William the Bastard
always got the job done.

William beat the Barons
at Caen in '47
with his allies, King and Pope
secure in earth and heaven.

William was only nineteen years
his first battle had been won
William the Bastard
got the job done.

William wed Mathilda
his relative by blood
against the teachings of the Church
in the power of his fierce love.

William knew Mathilda
she bore him a red-haired son
William the Bastard
got the job done.

William fought the King of France
and frustrated his great power
he fortified all Normandy
with motte and bailey tower.

Because William was a man of war
and when the combat's course was run
William the Bastard
got the job done.

William snared Earl Harold
and made him swear on holy bones
he'd give up his claim to England
and put him on the throne.

See, William had no scruple
he'd fuck you up for fun
William the Bastard
got the job done.

William triumphed in '66
you know how the story goes
he slaughtered England's finest
where the hoary apple-tree grows.

Three horses cut from under him
he cut down Godwinson
William the Bastard
got the job done.

In '69 Northumbria rose
against the Norman yoke
he butchered them – man, woman and child
until their resistance broke.

He knew the power of terror
of death and starvation
William the Bastard
got the job done.

William squeezed the English dry
a protection-racket crook
he wrote down principal and vig
in his loanshark Domesday Book.

A gangster and an asset-stripper
like monarchs every one
William the Bastard
got the job done.

William died in his bed in France
so fat from his Rachman plunder
that his coffin split as he lay in state
and his bowels burst asunder.

The earth would not accept him
and heaven him did shun
but William the Bastard
got the job done.

One of us

The good looking, charming man Margaret
always had a soft spot for, pinstripe smoothie
Cecil, with his boyish smile, brylcreemed hair,
and a side-parting to set your watch to.
A Carnforth railman's lad, hauled himself up
by his eh-bah-gum braces, grammar school,
Cambridge, millionaire, Tory MP.
Then Chairman of the Party v Arthur Scargill
on Question Time. King Arthur, the Cossack-quiffed
syndicalist from nah-then-lad Worsborough Dale,
President of the NUM via White Cross
Secondary Modern, Woolley Pit and the diehard
red-raggers of Yorkshire, the real Yorkshire,
where we lived, with pit tips, comprehensive schools
and sideburned Tetley bittermen,
not the sheep-spotted, cowpat Dales, beloved
of Southerners and the *Yorkshire Post*,
home of Tory farmers and fleece-topped
middle-class hikers; the real Yorkshire,
red or dead in tooth and claw,
in Docs and denims and donkey jackets,
the Yorkshire that flew into lines of coppers,
the Yorkshire that took down a Government;
there before us on TV, taking them down once more.
*'There are five points I'd like to make in response
to that frankly, preposterous assertion ...'*
– and in our flat South Riding vowels
he reeled them off, one after the other,
fluent as the Dearne, consonants blunt
as cobbles, arguments sharp as a diamond-bit,
each word a slap in the face, a punch
to the stomach, flustering Parkinson's
brilliantined cool, stammering
his learned RP. *One of us.* Inspired,
we were off, into CND, Anti-Nazi League

and the Socialist Workers Party,
NME reading fifth-formers, fighting fascists
in Leeds, selling papers on the market corner
debating Toryboy Hague on BBC Leeds,
taking to the streets in Blackpool,
Liverpool, London and Hull, for jobs,
against racism and nuclear missiles,
building barricades, daubing graffitos,
getting clubbed by the SPG: then '84,
the Alamo, labour's last stand: the call went out
and his people answered: Arthur Scargill,
we'll support you evermore.

The Ballad of Dave Hart

Dave Hart built a pyramid
in the grounds of Chadacre Hall
of limestone blocks with a golden tip
twenty-three feet tall.

Dave Hart built a pyramid
a family mausoleum
with tombs for thirty-four dead Harts
and a viewing point to see 'em.

Dave Hart built a pyramid
because he didn't want to croak
his life and works forgotten
like some ordinary bloke.

Dave Hart built a pyramid
a miniature pit stack
a gilded memento-mori
of the days of all-out attack.

Dave Hart built a pyramid
a monument to his finest hour
'The man who broke the NUM
and Arthur Scargill's power'.

Dave Hart built a pyramid
with a space for every member
of the National Working Miners Committee –
that is, if Dave remembers.

Dave Hart built a pyramid
a symbol of the occult scheming
of the Eton/Square Mile Croesus-class
poisoning England's dreaming.

Dave Hart built a pyramid
so his audacity could delight
his plutocrat, neo-con cronies
of the libertarian right.

Dave Hart built a pyramid
because the rich do as they please
break workers, destroy jobs and lives
at their pleasure, for their ease.

*David Hart, the multi-millionaire libertarian who organised the
back-to-work movement during the 1984-1985 Miners' Strike,
built a pyramid-shaped mausoleum in the grounds of his Suffolk
country house, Chadacre Hall. Hart died in 2011 and is
presumably interred therein.*

Nithing

I

Welcome to the Theatre of Hate.
Dramatis personae:

       Harold, the English King;
       William, Duke of Normandy;
       Arthur, President of the NUM;
       Ian, Chairman of the NCB, and;
       Margaret, Prime Minister of the United Kingdom of
       Great Britain and Northern Ireland.

II

nithing – **a.** hateful, *utlah*, beyond the pale; **b.** a being of
gratuitous malice, a gloater; **c.** sorcerer, poisoner, conjurer of
devils; **d.** deviant, perverse, taking the form of a woman; **e.**
traitor, perjurer, oathbreaker, liar; **f.** werewolf, lamprey, slow-
worm; **g.** cowardly, weak, one that slinks away; **h.** desiring anal
copulation; **i.** dickless, cocksucker, bitch, cunt, twat; **j.** *exlex*,
green-lit, one that must be killed.

III

Maggie Maggie Maggie
the nithing must be scolded
to force it to reveal

Ut Ut Ut
it seems to be a woman
and yet
an eelpout coils
in the slimy gusset

Every woman's got one
birther of werewolves
catfish and zander
Maggie Thatcher is one
hermaphrodite self-fucker
the lubricated head
of the butterfish
wriggling through the sphincter
Maggie Maggie Maggie

Ut Ut Ut

IV

what do you call a man with an hotel on his head? *norman tebbit*
anthony berry roberta wakeham muriel maclean eric taylor
jeanne shattock dead but margaret walked away clean five
minutes earlier she was reading wilbur smith on the shitter if it
had gone off then *just rejoice at that news* damn you patrick
mcgee *yorkshire miners yorkshire miners nah-nah-nah-nah-nah*

V

Will no one...
the first time
was on the A57 at Strines
midnight
werewolves on the moor
bummers in the public toilets
he was coming up from Ladybower
in his Jaguar
driving himself
his chauffeur absent at a family function
we knew
came flying over the brow of the hill
in the Cortina they stole for us

from the Alhambra Centre in Barnsley
and swerved into his path
his shredded wheat head
lit up in the headlights
his eyes flashed white
in the rear-view mirror
slewed into the heather
and almost rolled
before bouncing back onto the blacktop
tail-lights disappearing
over the hill to Sheffield
we looked at each other
pocketed our ice-picks

rid me...
the second time
we'd been drinking
feelings were running high
communist
traitor
utlah subversive
we drove down to Yews Lane
Freddie took a shot
through the front room window
we saw him flinch
then actually come forward
to the spiderweb glass
wondering what the hell was that
Freddie said *cheese it*
it was his own fucking car
imagine the blowback

of this turbulent ...
the third one came from MI5
via the CIA black book
Anton Cermak/Kennedy-squared
he was speaking at a rally in Mansfield
but we'd been working this patsy

through a cut-out
some dumbass scab
telling the world and his wife
he was going to rush the stage
and deck him with an iron bar
he was told a thousand times
headshot
headshot
headshot
headshot
swing it like a rounders bat
we provided the baton
got him to the front
and created a diversion
but Jesus he was thick
he tripped and dropped it
barely glancing his shoulder
before some flat-caps took him down
nithing patted down his hair
and kept on spouting
coal not dole

...priest
he'll curdle your milk
bring murrain on your cattle
fiddle with your children
rape the Queen Mother
anti-christ
wearg
commander of demons
may every man know his duty

VI

Shapeshifter
this thing with seeming valour
muscles and moustaches
adored by women
eager for battle
hauls knights from quicksands
then holds not to his word
harold sacramentvm fecit willelmo dvci
the broken bones of saints
willelm dedit haroldo arma
the broken ties of loyalty
treow sceal on eorle, wisdom on were
let all the people see
unvs clericus et aelfgyva
this cuckold and cuckolder
consecrated in Stigand's base oils
oathbreaker
nithing
utlah
exlex
let him be written from the record
the unclean lacuna
between the day King Edward
was alive and dead
and the crowning of treow King William

VII

macgregors beggars they named them for him this elderly
imported american from kinlochleven scion of a family of
paisleyite scabs going back to 26 she bought him to destroy them
he was champing at the bit straining at the leash they had to hold
him back he wanted to throw them all on the dole put them all
out on the streets a being of pure malice a mad dog *put the mad
dog down* the flambé chef at the wentbridge house hotel phoned
jeff and told him macgregors in the fleur de lys dining alone his
chauffeurs in the brasserie so they all went up there jeff scut
wally & jim they scarred the midnight blue of his bentley with
paint stripper slashed the tyres with stanley knives and scut
reached under his coat and pulled out a sawn-off and said i
could wait in the rhododendrons jeff told him dont be stupid
but scut was stoked and stocksmashed the drivers side window
they drove to that scabs house and shot out his windows

VIII

No man, but Mammon
conjured from Hell.
The Grasper, always wanting more
counting life and peoples as nought
stuffing his pockets
multiplying ledgers.

No man, but the Father of Lies.
Slanderer
coercer
perverter of oaths
racking and screwing
the golden bones of saints.

No man, but the whelp
of Grendel's mother
sucking hard
on the bitch tits of England,
a pot-bellied wolf-whelp
in image of Adam.

And the Northmen conspired
to slay him at Ferrybridge
and stake his undead body
in the fen at Hatfield Chase.

Guffaws spurted
through the heavens
like a hairy star:
the Aire ran blood
and parted.

No man, but fire;
a slavering she-wolf;
a wolverine's gullet;
Balberith's brute maw:
the day of his wrath has come
and who is able to stand?

Seditiones, caedem et rapinam

William forbade insurrections, killing and robbery,
thus restraining the people by arms and the arms by laws.

Ordericus Vitalis, *The Ecclesiastical History*

I

For the rind-white Frenchman
at the foot of the waycross
where Lound Lane forks to Rat Hall Farm
rubies crusting between his legs
walnut bollocks at the corners of his mouth
stripped cadaver
streaking like stilton –
forty six marks
from the Strafford wapentake.

For the dumped guts
and hacked-off hocks
of the butchered Hampole roebuck
tidal with worms
attended by crows and dancing magpies
in the full moon's halogen beam –
the gibbet at Stubbsbridge
the shotgunned long-dogs
two hundred pounds plus costs.

For the shattered face
of the bricksmashed
minibus driver
in the smoking ditch at Red House
the burned-down bungalow
on the Great North Road
the KO-ed cops at Frickley Athletic –
Axholme, Barnsdale
the Bridewell's biting irons.

II

and they trespassed in the private gardens at frickley hall
searching for fledglings fallen from the rookery and were
roughly seized by uncouth men who seemed to be english yet
worked in the pay of the foreign lord and they took them to him
and he chastised them with words that cut like glass and drove
them in his land rover to the police house at clayton and the
constable poured cherryade and took down their particulars and
they wiped away tears with the sleeves of their jumpers and
promised not to do it again on their way back one trespassed in
the gardens at frickley hall and found a fledgling fallen from the
rookery he stuffed it up his jumper and fled through the lit
rhododendrons

III

Silvaticus, phantom of the woods:
eluder of man-traps, evader of trip-wires,
master of shadows, crepuscular and fleet.

Gaitered in dew, belted with coneys,
dappled like the forest
in Jack Pyke Lincoln Green,
the pockets of his long coat
squirming with polecats:
lock-knife, hip-flask,
a crushed pack of Park Drive;
Wulfric, the one they call wild.

Hard voices in the forest
calling along the line.
Bootsnag treeroot, drystick breaking,
a cordon creeping forward.
Quarterpatch spaniels working the brambles,
whimpering and yelping, docked-tails whirring:

under bracken bank cover
swimming down into the loam
squeaking the garlic and spermy bluebells,
breathing woodlice and centipedes,
willing himself to a mossy hummock –

a palm held flat, a straight arm pointing:
the mauling mouths of mastiffs
plunging at the nape.

The gibbet by the high road.
Marten, magpie, wildcat, owl.
Eyeless, thumb-dangled infants.
Villeins lopped and opened,
choking on venison tongues.

From the tracks and byways the mute woods speak.
STRICTLY PRIVATE
NO ADMITTANCE
DANGER TO DOGS
TRESPASSERS WILL BE PROSECUTED.
But from Thorn Covert, Mappleyard
and Hooton Wood,
they took back their treasure:
partridge, woodcock, pheasant and hare;
scribbler and whitethroat, the rooty cups of jays.

IV

the day we caught a mole under the bridge by watchley farm this
muckspreading posh kid leapt from his tractor and screamed at
us incoherent interpreted meaning get off my land he was bigger
and older but there were three of us and he looked and sounded
like a puff someone muttered fuck off and we carried on walking
he leapt over the stream said im talking to you are you deaf as
well as stupid and pushed stanley in the chest words were
exchanged some punches stanley dared me to joyride in the
tractor but we were in deep enough already we cut across the
cornfield to the disused railway sprinting all the way when we
got to the main road at moorhouse we took off our jackets and
whenever a car passed ducked behind the hedges we didnt relax
until we were back in the wimpeys it didnt make calendar or the
south yorkshire times and the knock never came but even so we
gave the park a miss for the rest of that summer

V

In Durham and York
the twin vernaculars
of fire and steel
translated
fitzRichard
and Comines
to hell.

Baz *nithing*
defied his red rose exile
and came to Sherwood.
He commando-crawled
the mist-wreathed cornfield
to fell
the bullhorn scabherd.

In three nights
Jas Goff and Len Spencer
pulled thirty rainbows
from Aldam's pool,
five dozen pheasants
from his pen at Hooton Wood,
three hares,
a muntjac
and a vanful of coneys.
They pinned a thank you
on the beech stump
by the rusting wheelbarrow.

quietly
beneath the contempt
of the *Observer* magazine
they live little lives
by privet and playing fields
libraries and supermarkets
papershops and swimming baths
walking dogs
washing cars
and watching tv
drinking at the bar in the Empire Club on Sundays
waiting for the turn.

Ballad of the Scabs

In '72 the NUM
shook the Tory State
closing down the cokeworks
there at Saltley Gate.

The miners' flying pickets
and their comrades in the TUC
showed the power the workers have
when they act in unity.

In '74 they finished the job
and forced out Edward Heath
they chipped in from their pay rise
to buy capital a wreath.

The ruling class got nervous
and planned a counter-attack
to perpetate their power
and put the workers on the rack.

The Tory Party, Eton School
Garrick Club and Whites
M15 and the CBI
Earls and Dukes and Knights;

Oxbridge Universities
Fleet Street and the BBC
Scotland Yard and Whitehall
and the Royal family,

Put their heads together
class warriors to a man
dispensed with pretence of democracy
and adopted the Ridley Plan.

Stockpile a year's supply of coal
burn nukes and North Sea gas
let striking miners' families starve
no DHSS brass.

Jackboot up the coppers
unleash Special Branch and spies
informers and provocateurs
propaganda lies.

Suspend civil liberties
occupy their towns
the colonial ploy of divide and rule
will bring the miners down.

See, the ruling class know who they are
and what they are there for
to run Britain for their benefit
within or without the law.

Would it that the workers
saw things just as clear
and recognised their interests
free of fog and fear.

Thatcher beat Jim Callaghan
in 1979
with a secret, backdoor plan
to close down half the mines.

But Arthur Scargill saw it true
and said it loud and clear
they'll destroy our jobs and communities
within a single year.

The lads ragged out at Brampton
when they threatened Cortonwood
pickets flew throughout the coalfield
like both sides knew they would.

The pits stopped work in Scotland
Durham and South Wales too
Kent and the Yorkshire area
were solid through and through.

But in Nottingham and Derby
the pit head gear kept turning
incentive pay and false promises
had kept the lads from learning,

That they could never trust the bosses
they fell for divide and rule
Your pits are safe for fifty years
the Tories played them for a fool.

They bussed them through the picket lines
through hails of broken slabs
Ian MacGregor's beggars
Margaret Thatcher's scabs.

They drew their wages every week
they said, 'I'm alright Jack.
Who cares if they shut down Cortonwood?
We won't get the sack.'

Col Clark scabbed at Pye Hill
John Liptrot at Sherwood Pit
they said they had the right to work
that they would not submit,

To 'Scargill's Marxist bully-boys
vile intimidation'
they founded the Working Miners' Group –
class traitor their vocation.

Chris Butcher scabbed at Bevercotes
they called him Silver Birch
he took Thatcher's thirty pieces
and left his comrades in the lurch.

Ken Foulstone scabbed at Manton
his mate Bob Taylor too
the Tories took them to one side
and told them what to do.

They went for lunch with David Hart
at Claridges Hotel
and agreed to sue their union
over *foie gras* and Cristal.

Sir Hector Laing stumped up some cash
Lord Hanson stumped up more
they served a writ on Scargill
on the Labour Conference floor.

A firm of Tory lawyers
deployed the state machine
and outlawed Scargill and the NUM
to the silence of the TUC.

See, all those bastards need to win
is Brotherhood to fail
in cringing fear of state assault
of courts and fines and jail.

Scab lawsuit on scab lawsuit
bound the Exec up in knots
Hart's 'Gulliver strategy' –
tie off the head, the body rots.

Autumn turned to winter
and the State intransigent
resolved to force the union
back to work without settlement

The pickets kept on up turning up
at the back lanes to the pits
but each month more weak and desperate
gave up the fight and quit.

They drove them through the picket lines
in mesh-windowed Black Marias
faces hidden behind scarves
untouchables, pariahs.

The half-bricks and the insults flew
the ritual push and shove
but the scab vans made it to the pit
to receive the Gaffer's love.

Down there in the Midlands though
scabs strolled in through the gates
bold as brass, in thousands
flashing V-signs at their mates.

They founded a management union
the so-called UDM
scab-led by Lynk and Prendergast
against the NUM.

They called them freedom fighters
for 'jobs and democracy'
but they were class-collaborators
conned by the duplicity,

Of their boss-class puppet-masters –
they've no care for the working man –
but in the race for power and profits
they'll lie and scheme and scam.

So the strike began to founder
dim prospect of success
and though the men stayed strong and dignified
long months of distress

Led them back without a settlement
to the spite of the NCB;
Thatcher ordered, 'kid gloves off'
and took an axe to the industry.

And were the scabs then happy
with their 'guaranteed' Midlands jobs
after twelve rich months of overtime
and hanging out with nobs?

'They said that we were heroes
they'd give us a parade
for saving the British coal industry
from Scargill's hair pomade.'

They thought the Tories were their friends
but how were they deceived
within ten years their pits were shut
their villages bereaved.

Pye Hill closed in '85
Sherwood '92
Bevercotes in '93
the things those Tories do.

Manton closed in '94
and by 1995
there were only sixteen deep-mine pits
in the country still alive.

And in the towns and villages
in the shadow of the dark pit stack
was dole and dereliction
and epidemic smack.

So Colin Clark, John Liptrot
where are your rich friends now?
Hart and Laing and Hanson
that twin-set Sacred Cow?

And Foulstone, Butcher, Taylor
how's your job for life?
What was it exactly the UDM
promised, in place of strife?

And the moral of this story
don't trust rich parasites
who hold in contempt the working man
be prepared to stand and fight.

Don't be seduced by bribery
their flattery or your greed
stay true to your comrades and your class:
the war is won by unity.

1069

I fell upon the English of the Northern shires
like a ravening lion.

Guillaume, Duc de Normandie

All England was surgent, murmurous
under the Frenchman's yoke. The geld was heavy,
the insults unbearable; expropriation,
partial judgement, the exemplary slaughter
of those who dared protest. Dispossessed helots
in their occupied land. Hostages hung
from the walls of red cities, burned farmsteads,
smashed watermills, disembowelled kine;
gullible Saxon thegns disarmed
by lies of restoration to their lands.

But the North had not submitted
and the people dreamed of mastery
in their land. The Northumbrian fyrd
rallied behind Waltheof and the Aetheling,
Cospatrick, Maerleswein and Siward Barn.
Osbjorn came to Humber with many ships,
and, emboldened, the Northmen rose,
slaying the oppressor at Durham and at York.
They chased the French to Trent's broad valley,
and urged the Mercians rise.

The Mercians rose and the Frenchman crushed them.
Guillaume marshalled his forces and rode North.
He bought off Osbjorn and bribed Malcolm of Scots
to harry Waltheof on the borders.
The Northmen held him at Aire for three weeks,
but once he'd forced the crossing they dared not
meet him, scattering to forest and fen.
Guillaume bore Harold's crown to York
and the Northern thegns prostrated: he resolved
to teach them a lesson in blood.

Throughout the iron-hard Northumbrian winter,
Norman death-squads prowled, slaughtering
greybeards and smooth-cheeked boys, raping mothers
and daughters, razing manors and hamlets,
granaries and packed tithe barns. Screaming
thumbscrews gave up outlaws from mountain
and fell; sword-edge bled resistance white:
this North would provision the rebel fyrd
no more, no longer the springboard
of Danish ambition be.

Guillaume returned south to the venison
hundreds, Winchester, Westminister.
In the northern wapentakes, the peasants
gnawed dog bones and scratted for threadbare plantain,
as their Lords conspired to accommodate,
with de Bully, de Mortain and Alain,
Compte de Bretagne, cringing to mortgage
their servile manors, desert and depopulate,
written in Domesday's blood: *Warram, wasta;
Warter, wasta; Wetwang, wasta; Wichum, wasta...*

Wasta

Gordon Place and Oxford Street, South Elmsall;
boarded up terraces, skyholed smoking roofs;
copper pipe and hot water tanks stripped out,
crackheads and smackrats moved in.

Absentee landlords picked up the lot
at auction, '93; six grand per run-down unit.
A no maintenance free-for-all,
DSS tenants, state-assured profit.

No questions asked: evicted council
and HA tenants from Newcastle,
Lincoln, Norwich and Hull, runners
from something, neighbours-from-hell.

Strange accents in Twiby's newsagents
and the obvious question – why on earth
would a jobless Geordie move to Elmsall,
and choose to live on Oxford Street?

We can guess; he knew someone from the nick
or met a bird when he worked at Butlins,
a single mother, desperate for attention
with a couple of brayed and neglected kids.

But it wasn't just the incomers;
feral flotsam from a five-mile radius –
the disordered, unparented, unemployable –
homed in with their hand-to-mouth heroin chaos.

Within a year, it happened, chronicled
in disbelieving eyes and the *Hemsworth Express*;
pensioners mugged and murdered, the methadone rapist,
shotgun drug wars and endemic burglary.

A 'former mining village', where retired
colliers cower at the knock on the door;
a 'close knit community', where futureless
losers booze 10am Special Brew,

and throw their empty cans and insults
at the scandalised white-haired ladies,
waiting in the bus stop, talking of happier days,
when young men worked and the pit was open.

A sin and a shame

for Craig Emerson

From the summit of Broad Lane tip,
over-looking the path to Frickley Park
and the York to Sheffield railway line,
we watch the demolition crews taking down
the pit.
                    The washery and beltways,
with their kestrel eyrie, are levelled already.
The lamproom, its roof-full of pipistrelles,
bulldozed flat. The canteen, where on the way back
from nesting, a kid could get a pasty
and a lukewarm bottle of pop, and the offices,
with their mown and clippered gardens,
neat privet, cherry trees and thrush-spotted lawns:
heaps of smoking rubble.
                                        The twin towers
of the winding gear remain, until,
at the time appointed in the *Hemsworth Express*,
a camcorder crowd gathers on the field
at the back of our houses, to see dynamite
bring them down. The button is duly pressed,
and through the rumbling dust, the horizon
is clear to Hooton Pagnell for the first time
in a hundred years.
                            Some muted 'whoos',
then shaken heads and silence. Your Uncle Frank
turns his back – *well, that's it then* – and shuffles off
along the path to Bradley Carr Terrace,
the path my Grandad trod each Friday,
to join the queues at the wages windows
and pick up his fifteen pound and change.
Thousands used to work here.
                                        You turn your face

from the obliterated place, at which
you used to work, and tell me again –
it's a sin and shame. There are no more words.
As the crowd and security drift away,
we walk up the hill and onto the pit,
across the barren place where, you delighted
upon last year, the nest I told you
was a little ringed plover's.

Search and Destroy

*1984*Abercynon Abernant Aberpergwm Abertillery Ackton Hall Agecroft Allerton Bywater Annesley Arkwright Ashington Askern Babbington Baddesley Bagworth Barnburgh Barnsley Main Barony Bates Bearpark Bedwas Bentinck Bentley Bersham Betteshanger Betws Bickershaw Bilston Glen Birch Coppice Bilsthorpe Blaenant Blidworth Bold Bolsover Brenkley Brookhouse Cadeby Cadley Hill Calverton Clipstone Comrie Cortonwood Cotgrave Coventry Creswell Cronton Cwm Cynheidre Darfield Dawdon Daw Mill Dearne Valley Deep Navigation Denby Grange Dinnington Donnisthorpe Easington Ellington Ellistown Emley Moor Eppleton Ferrymoor Riddings Florence Frances Frickley Fryston Garw Gascoigne Wood Gedling Glasshoughton Goldthorpe Grimethorpe Haig Harworth Hem Heath Herrington Hickleton Holditch Horden Houghton Main Kilnhurst Kinsley Kiveton Park Lady Winsor LeaHall Ledston Luck Linby Littleton Longannet Maltby Mansfield Manton Manvers Margam Marine Markham Markham Main Merthyr Vale Monktonhall Moor Green Murton Nantgarw Newstead North Selby Nostell Oakdale Ollerton Parkside Penallta Penrhiwceiber Point of Ayr Polkemmet Polmaise Prince of Wales Pye Hill Rawdon Renishaw Park Riccall Rossington Royston Rufford Sacriston Savile Seafield Seaham Sharlston Sherwood Shirebrook Shireoaks Silverdale Silverhill Silverwood Six Bells Snowdown South Kirkby South Leicester Steetley Stillingfleet StJohns Sutton Sutton Manor Taff Merthyr Thurcroft Tilmanstone Treeton Treforgan Trelewis Tower Vane Tempest Warsop Wath Main Wearmouth Welbeck Westoe Wheldale Whittal Whitwell Whitwick Winsor Wistow Wolstanton Woolley Yorkshire Main *[Hatfield Kellingley?Thoresby?]***2015**

Objective One

Through the mists of an April dawn
a crowd flowed along Manvers Way, so many,
I had not thought the dole had undone so many,
sending them herded from the fuming valleys
of Dearne and Dove and Don and Rother,
into the bus bays and car parks of Ventura,
ASOS and Next PLC, where they pour
from Nissans, Vauxhalls and private hire minicabs,
lighting cigarettes, adjusting iPhones,
pressing mobiles to their ears, striding out
in polished patent, pinstripes breaking
on the buckled instep, tailored skirts
and long coats flaring on the breeze.

Sixty thousand work here, in logistics,
call-centres, light industry and retail,
along the roundabouted blacktop
from Birdwell to Barnsdale, the EU funded
M1 to A1 link road. Objective One,
bringing light to parochial darkness,
access, investment, enterprise, jobs;
until sterling collapses, Kolkata undercuts
and the market-zeitgeist lurches,
retrenching capital in gold and gilts
and the provincia flips once more
to wrecking-ball brownfield-bombsite,
the full monty of dole and dereliction,
where brassed-off, hand-to-mouth yokels
are abandoned to dearth and absurdity,
their eh-bah-gum tutu dreams.

Once there were woods and open fields,
fens in the flatland, villages on the hill.
Bullheads in the millstream, polecats
in the warren; red kite, raven, white-tailed eagle,
over the wolf-prowled heath. Danelaw sokeland,
assarted from wildwood, torp in the langthwaite clays;
the Anglecynn muster at Ringstone Hill,
where three wapentakes meet; Oswald's grange
by the holy well – belltower, gatehouse,
carucates for geld. Here, beyond Whitwell
and the five boroughs, beyond Mercia's
clement mid-lands, we will beat the bounds
at rogationtide from Bamburgh, Danum,
Durham and York; the dragon-prowed river,
the waycross on the roman road, hoar apple tree,
whit's gospel thorn, the tumulus at Askern Hill;
these are the roots that clutch, these the sprouting corpses,
these are the fragments, I shore against my ruins.

Mongrel Blood Imperium

Too near the ancient troughs of blood
Innocence is no earthly weapon.

Geoffrey Hill,
'Ovid in the Third Reich'

The Territory

What is intended?

Mongrel-blood imperium (a),
that is, an empire
of mixed, or hybrid,
perhaps even 'degenerate',
'race' ('ethnicity'?)?

Or,
mongrel-blood imperium (b),
as above, but the imputed 'mongrels'
of the *hoi polloi*
governed for their good
by a caste of pedigree brahmins?

Or,
mongrel blood-imperium,
a 'racial' or 'ethnic' empire
of a single… 'blood' ('people'?, 'race'?)
somehow 'sullied' (undermined, devalued, compromised)
by … miscegenation, immigration, globalisation?

Surely not?

Perhaps a backhanded affirmation, *nigga*,
appropriating the discourse of the oppressor [sic]
queering their deal
'our' (relativist, libertarian, pink, oppositional) way,
spiking the Maxims
with lilies and rainbows?

Hmmm.
Suspect in origin
something more callow,
concatecated concepts
of nitro-glycerine glamour,
a logorrheic Luitpoldarena,
Generation Terrorists,
Che t-shirt and camouflage combats:
an unnecessary, misunderstandable, glib
PROVOCATION

        nevertheless
        marking the territory.

Get your interest?

Four Nations

Archaeology's blur of supposition
attributes flint-knapped debitage
in antique Suffolk alluvium
to Homo heidelbergensis
circa 700,000 years ago:
the first five-toed feet in ancient times
to walk Atlantic's green peninsula.

Interglacial emerald
thaws to moated archipelago.
In the stratified silts
of spelunked Creswell,
equine brain-pans,
marrowless femurs of caprid and bos,
chipped Neanderthal ribcage:
Solutrean spearheads
disarticulating vertebrae –

heeeere's Johnny!

We know the pre-literate progression;
palaeo, meso, neo.
But from Creswell to Kents, Starr Carr
to Hengeworld's 'ritual' landscape,
the tendentious fantasias
of nerdish yearning
are everything we have –
next to nothing.

Fast forward then
to the relative certainties of ink on vellum,
Pytheas via Strabo, and noble Tacitus,
naming Catevellauni,
Ordivices, Brigantes,
congenial Belgae fled from Gaul –
twin-tongued Pretanni,
for want of a better term, *Celts*.

Polyglot legions of Aulus;
Agricola following.
Swart Cyrenaiceans
of Septimus Severus,
pumping dark DNA
into the milky genepool.
Romans go home,
incipit Hengist and Horsa;
ethnic cleansing and interbreeding,
paler pirates from the North
spunking the sceptred brood-bitch.

                              That'll do for now.

Bede's four nations.
More or less the fair field, more or less the folk;
there was an Englishman, an Irishman
and a Scotsman; (the Welshman absent,
no doubt fettling his sheep).

It's the way I tell 'em.

                              But now we can start.

Acts of Union

Rejecting promiscuous
metaphors of congress,
instead I meditate
on the transactional
crudities of power.
Anglo-Saxons twisting
the arms of Celts
until they agreed
to sign over the deeds;
the elites of four nations
gerrymandering title
and banking the rental.
Because we are busy
watching the X Factor,
being trained for vocational literacy
in our outstanding schools
and world-class universities,
stroking strangers on Facebook
or simply slaughtering 'Pakis'
on our various Calls of Duty,
we have no time to remember
the Laws in Wales Acts
1535 and 1542,
Cromwell's tender annexation,
1707, 1801
and the almost Civil
and very uncivil WAR!
that half undid the last.
Fail, Gael and Sinn Fein.
SNP, Plaid Cymru –
the *English Democrats*?
Rosyth rhetoric,
Atlantic oil and gas,
tautologous taglines –
'Independence in Europe'.

Despite Olympics
and Orangemen,
the settlement slowly unravelling?
Signed bits of paper,
steel that scythes down men.
Ballot-box and blood.

Krákumál

From Greenland to Gadarike,
hairy-arsed Ragnar
furrowed the fulmar's field,
sword-edge blade-bite
and bone-breaking battleaxe
won the foam-paved whale-road.
Profit he had in plenty
prestige in peril and plunder:
insensate sons, savage and implacable
as dog star's howling ocean.

We smote them with swords!
The beserks of Aslaug's wolf-whelps
fluttered the flaps of England's bitches
on the blood-reddened rushes
of butchered halls.
Hvitserk, Ironside, Snake-in-the-Eye,
and worm-legged Ivar, king.
Widowed-wombs whelmed
with the seed of Sigurd,
brigandage in the blood.

We coshed them with cannon!
Sharking the sea-lanes
with sharp-prowed ships
stand-and-delivering Argentine silver
down the broadside barrels
of three pound falcons.
Drake, Hawkins, White,
privateers, a parsimonious
parliament's proxy for war
outsourced to pirates and chancers.

We destroyed them with Debt!
The state hocked to shylocks
to spare rich men taxation
and underwrite their wars.
Rich men also being the shylocks,
getting paid from both ends.
The lives of private soldiers
pawned to profiteers. Death's dividends,
raising fleets and country houses,
confirming capital's coup d'état.

We blasted them with broadsides!
The gouted gourmands
of Brooks's and Boodle's,
Empire's intrepid investors,
vote conquest for corners, cartels.
The First Rate hundred-gunners
of columned Horatio
enforcing transactions
on favourable terms
to Westminster's global land grab.

We gloried in gouache!
Dyce's nude crudity,
a wet dream of naked naiads
and trumpeting beefcake,
Neptune resigning to pomped Britannia
the Empire of the Sea.
Feargus O'Connor, eight million
grass-eating Taigs are amazed
at the bare-arsed cheek
of Mercury's Phrygian cap.

We abased them with alliteration!
Christianity, commerce and civilisation:
conquest, I presume?
Rhodes visioned dominion
from Cairo to the Cape,
red-inking Mercator's monochrome
mapbook. White-gloved house-boys
serving Fino and Victoria sponge;
squatting in the dirt,
eating sadza with their fingers.

We fragged them with freedom!
Punjab voted with fire
and steel. Matabeleland
massacres, progress
to cholera and internet fraud.
Empire's orphans, half-savage,
half-child, nostalgic for a future
of tiffin and the Telegraph;
Lord Curzon carrying on:
up the Khyber.

We routed them with relativism!
Xhosa forced out San.
Zulu crushed Xhosa.
Blood River, Ulundi; (Sharpeville,
Soweto): AIDS in a bobble hat.
It's never black and white;
all men take pleasure
in peril and plunder - in power;
if a man can, he will:
all that's lacking is the means.

From the corbelled snake-pit,
Ragnar sang fair Kraka's lay.
Aelle's sun-conjured fang-worms
hung off his naked stilton,
zigzag shreds of his own inked skin.
Hildr's blurred wings closing,
eyes opening to Valholl.
Avenging Ivar sails ocean's curve
to slaughter, loot and burn:
the roaring benches praise him in the song.

Irish Blood, English Heart

Is there anybody here with, uh, any Irish in them? [Cheers]
Is there any of the girls'd like a little more Irish in them? [More cheers]

Phil Lynott, introducing 'Emerald' on the Thin Lizzy album, *Live and Dangerous*.

I

Blood's obfuscations
crimson our vision.
Yet the narrative's clear.
One way: occupation,
colonisation, annexation – *genocide*?
The other, resistance,
'the vomit surge of hate',
the refugee road of emigration and exile.
And yet …

The wisdom of Dublin's booted Arthur:

just because a man is born in a stable,
it doesn't make him a horse.

Spenser and Sweet Sir Walter
in the Munster Plantation.
Mad Dog and King Rat
from the Scot-sown Shankill.
Leonard Healaighe,
Lord Mayor of turretted Pomfret
in the dying years
of the planter Queen.

Imperial hubris
self-undermining,
Act of Union giving voice
to Home Rule and secession.
Duelling Danny took Clare
and choked on the Oath of Supremacy:
incipit Catholic Emancipation
courtesy of *England's* Iron Duke.

> Con Markiewicz recused at Lissadell,
> at Long Kesh, Bobby Sands.

The elephantine memory
of Ian Richard Kyle Paisley
First Minister of Northern Ireland,
MP for North Antrim 1970-2010,
also remembers 1829
the predestined elect
rehabilitate with Antichrist:

> *trick or treat?*

William Butler Yeats
of the Irish Republican Brotherhood,
scion of the Protestant Ascendancy.
Sir Roger Casement,
British Consul to the Belgian Congo & Peru,
Knight Companion of the Order of St. Michael and St. George,
Sinn Fein and Irish Volunteer.
Vol. Francis Hughes
painter and decorator
Brit-killing brigand of the Armagh badlands.

The remnant of Uí Néill's
emerald Gaeltacht
pressed to Atlantic
from Donegal to Dingle
speaking Sky Sports
and Coronation Street.
The six counties
fluent in Bogside's hooped demotic:

>   *oo-ah up the 'RA, say oo-ah up the 'RA*
>   *oo-ah up the 'RA, say oo-ah up the 'RA*

Peter Brady
son of Matt Brady of Óglaigh na hÉireann
and May Caffrey of Cumann na mBan
bit out his alien, native tongue
and cast off his natal, alien identity
rebirthing as Ruairí Ó Brádaigh
in the peopled living stream.

English, language of the Irish –
Montague, Mahon, Muldoon.
Irish, 'pigs' of the English –
(John Junor's foul condescension
when 30,000 enfranchised 'Brits'
elected Robert Gerard Sands
M.P. for Fermanagh and South Tyrone) –
Erin's peasanted kernes
being the grunts bearing the brunt
of Westminster's imperial wars
in shamrocked foreign fields
from Bengal to Bloemfontein,
Salamanca to Sevastapol.

Yet the 'chestnut-tree, great-rooted blossomer'
blighted with spore-borne fungal rot
from the unrelenting easterly
still drops her hard-headed sons and daughters
in the currents of Empire's ocean,
still finding harbour
in England's amnesiac strands.

II

The poster in the window
of the Railway Hotel
advertises a heavyweight bout:
'Leo 'the Irishman' Mulhern
vs Gypsy Joe Gorman.
The tautologous tagline –
'this Irishman really comes to fight'
sums up his slugger's style.
Maisie's son and
heir of nothing
but his fighting blood,
out of Cambridge Street, Moorthorpe,
in the heart of the Yorkshire coalfield,
via Hackney and raw Donegal.
Homed from home,
in the red-brick Irish enclave
terraced around St. Joe's.

Irish? We knew them as 'Catholics' only,
each morning as we dawdled to school
in our docs and denims and Simon shirts,
they'd be waiting for the bus
to scary St. Wilfrid's
in blazers, ties and provocative saffron shirts.
Taig-exoticism aside,
the thought that our friends,
enemies and team-mates
were anything other than just-like-us,
never crossed our minds
as we common-koined
in Yorkshire brogue,
thee and *tha* and come *Come on England!*,
with Tighes and Tullys,
Bradleys and D'Arcys,
Kellys, O' Reillys,
McGowans and Burkes –

> Mark Murtagh and Chris Curry,
> dashing right and left wings
> of Kirkby's Boys' Brigade;
> Finns, Walshes and Mullans
> in Upton's brawling
> champ thirteen;
> Mick O'Brien and Kev Malley
> of the Parachute Regiment,
> Derry, Longden and Belize;
> Dennis Doody of UCATT and the SWP,
> 'unconditional but critical support';
> Patrick Tighe of the NUM
> and South Kirkby Miners' Welfare;
> Joe Connell of Keble
> and the Inns of Court;
> Mick Brogan of the 100 Club
> and the Gang of Four road crew;
> Kev Barry, smackhead and nonce;
> Philomena Geraldina Teresa Anne Savage.

Advance one hundred and ninety years.
Pat Mulhern and Jayne Ely
at St. Joseph's altar,
coupled in the rite
joining squint-eyed Sihtric
and Ealdgyth of Wessex
a thousand years before them.
ego conjungo vos in matrimoniam.

Remember in vision
the marqueed reception,
before The Birdie Song.
but after The Snake,
Stephen Morrissey
swinging the mike and singing:

> *Irish blood, English heart, this I'm made of*
> *There is no one on earth I'm afraid of.*

The blood-dipped rose
efflorescing from emerald sepals.

Camp Fire Yarn No. 28

Mop your platters with bannocks, soak-up every stain and scrap
of God's grace of bacon and beans, then sit up straight-backed,
hands folded in lap, 'round the fire where the billy-can sings:
and I'll tell of Colonel Baden Powell and the Siege of Mafeking.

Kruger's crude and boorish Boers had massed against Natal
and meant to annex old England's earth to their insolent Transvaal.
Our troops outnumbered and outgunned from building Empire on the cheap:
the Queen called for bold Impresa – 'the wolf that never sleeps'.

From loyal Rhodesia B.P. enrolled a regiment of horse
and garrisoned civilian Mafeking with a patched-together force
of Bechuana riflemen, yeomen from the town,
police and a teenaged cadet-corps – boys of pluck and great renown.

It was a feint to draw the Boers away from the Navy's ironclad coasts
because it was from Port Natal we'd reinforce with stout redcoats
who'd drive the unwashed Afrikaans back to their kaffired farms:
a siege behind his rebel lines would tie Kruger's forces down.

But cut off from ordnance and supply, alone on the kopjed wold
B.P. knew he'd have to improvise if Mafeking was to hold.
He dug miles of sandbagged trenches, built gun-emplacements, towers
sent scouts and spies, set guards at vigil, in the panther-prowled small
   hours.

Smiths forged guns and bayonet blades, of cold, hard Sheffield steel
and B.P. rationed food and water and brought the beasts in from the field.
He maintained morale with cheery drills, and a Sunday cricket match
theatre, sports and Empire's feasts, under the Union Jack.

Field glasses glinted from the rocks surrounding the valiant town,
as Kruger pried for weaknesses that might bring the garrison down.
But B.P. was a fox as well as wolf and he gulled those unread Boers
into thinking the jerry-built garrison invulnerable to their corps.

But the gun emplacements were mostly fake, the barbed-wire, knotted string
the khakied troops civilians, those 'ladies' at the spring,
casually drawing water in the sights of sniper-spies –
the brave boys of the cadet corps in pigeon-breast disguise.

At last October brought the day when Kruger declared his war,
sending Cronje and eight thousand Boers to batter at Mafeking's door.
B.P.'s two thousand were not dismayed – let the Boers come if they dared:
for the sleepless wolf had schooled his cubs and they were well prepared.

Four to one's the kind of odds at which no Englishman should despair
and even when bombs and mortar-shells were shrieking through the air
blasting bodies to kingdom come and the trenches running with blood
each man did his duty, as each man knew he should.

Sometimes it seemed by force of men the Boers would over-run
the threadbare khaki and fallen walls of the hard-pressed garrison.
But every time a breach seemed near, ranks of unsheathed-steel
swarmed to push the devils back, forcing them to yield.

For seventeen and two hundred days Mafeking held out
against artillery and siege-works, snipers and hellish drought.
Eight hundred dead and wounded, down to gruel and bully beef
still Empire's ragged standard flew, until Mahon brought Relief.

Church bells rang across our lands, the packed streets danced mad flings
of joy at the deeds of bold B.P. and the heroes of Mafeking.
Those fellows were no funkers, although most were tenderfoots:
each man did his duty, showing nerve and pluck and guts.

They fought for country and for Queen, and for Almighty God
in the name of England's Empire, for every stone and sod
bought, conquered, bartered, found-anew, annexed to Britannia's realm
on which the sun can never set, and never be overwhelmed.

The Zulu sang Impresa's name, Xhosa and Bushman too
every black man in the Cape, from Kimberley to Karoo,
for the Boer holds the kaffir as less than a dog, to be beaten and enslaved
branded as Cain and outcast made, predestined to be unsaved.

But Britain brought them church and school, work and infirmary
and redeemed them from their double-bond of slavery and idolatry.
Sneering reds and lesser breeds proclaim Empire 'piracy':
but wherever flies the Union Flag, is law and liberty.

So my lads, open your hearts and learn Mafeking's lesson well,
because on his honour each English boy should promise that he will
do his duty to God, and to his Queen, and to every fellow man
and be counted in the fray, so all might say – he's a true-born Englishman.

Ely on Orwell on Eliot on Kipling

I know of no writer of such great gifts for whom poetry seems to have been purely an instrument.

T.S. Eliot, *A Choice of Kipling's Verse*

Kipling is … morally insensitive and aesthetically disgusting … and yet there is much [of his poetry] that is capable of giving pleasure to people who know what poetry means.

George Orwell, *Essays*

Eliot, evasive, uneasy in his judgements;
in defending Kipling from accusations
of fascism, also defending his compromised self
from similar besmirching. Philistine
and aesthete, jingo imperialist
and reactionary anti-Semite, twin tendencies
leading to Mosley. Orwell, despite Eton
and the Colonial Service, rude-rooted
in England and the working man, using crude Rudyard
to unnerve Eliot and club the 'pansy left'.
But both on the button with their evaluations:
Eliot's great-gifted journalist of topical verse,
art subdued to its instrument; Orwell's
tabloid sentimentalist and 'good bad poet'.

Note how both denied him the title 'poet',
Eliot explicitly, Orwell in effect; a 'bad poet',
even a 'good' one, being barely a poet at all.
His ballads, full rhyme and rum-ti-tum rhythms
transgressed the canons of allusive
modernity and bludgeoned tentative lyric
with certain assertion. Popularity, too
is disqualification; the sanctimonious truths
of 'If', for example, chime in suburbia
like the *Sunday Express*, as 'Gunga Din's' racism
echoes in the golf club bar. Yet still
he endures, firing schoolboy imagination
with the brutal adventure of England's Empire,
lurid as music hall, compelling as comics.

Inglan is a bitch

Noh mattah wat dey say,
come wat may,
we are here to stay
inna Inglan.

Linton Kwesi Johnson, 'It Dread Inna Inglan (For George Lindo)', *Dread Beat an' Blood.*

1. Boxing Day, 1979

For Jim Nightingale, in memory of John Clark

Having pissed away our Christmas money
getting under-age hammered in the Plough,
Red Jim's party in Centre Street called.
Clarky got the invite through their Col,
a combat-jacketed, Trotskyite journo
who worked for the *Sheffield Star*. We were punks,
two years too late, as early as we could get there,
angry, attitudinal, raw with unfocused rebellion:
ripe for evangelisation.

                             Dread Beat an' Blood
was shaking down the walls from fifty yards
away. The door opened to laughter
and spurting lager, a smell I guessed was dope.
Strange things were afoot: the front room was postered
like Wolfie Smith's bedroom – like *my* bedroom –
Marx and Marley, the stencilled fist

from Power in the Darkness; men
wearing suit-coats over jeans and t-shirts,
women casually bra-less in loose-knit
mohair sweaters; lit candles in wine bottles;
people actually drinking wine, from TV's
long-stemmed glasses. 'Beer Mon?' from the kitchen –
a *real-life rasta,* handing out Heineken.
And in the ransacked pantry, the night's
stunning revelation – a yard long pack
of Buitoni spaghetti, exotic
as absinthe.
              Who lives in a house like this?
We cornered the cans and set to supping
at the kitchen table, where at length
Jim found us, and put us through our paces,
discussing the Clash and TRB,
Trident, Thatcher and the National Front,
before finally getting down to it –
Marx and revolution. Softened up
by Clarky's *Socialist Workers* and Neil Spencer's
pink *NME*, we weren't found wanting.
We signed on the line and a fortnight later,
boarded the bus to Cas Civic Centre
for our first live gig: Rock Against Racism,
the Mekons with Galaxy supporting.
Galaxy were disco, four handsome black men
in sequined shirts pastiching Kool and the Gang.
Col Clark clenched his fist in solidarity
and shouted at the soundcheck – 'Dillinger!
Big Youth!' The lead singer grinned and shook his head –
'We're R&B mon, we don't do reggae!'

Some beer-guts in flares crashed the concert
to kick-off with the freaks. Skinny socialists
converged and battered them out of the exits.
It was an eye-opener.
                          The paper every week,
'Support the Steel Workers, General Strike Now';
The monthly journal, International Socialism,
'Lessons from the Revolution in Iran';
Anti-Nazi League pamphlets, 'The National Front
is a Nazi Front, Smash the National Front':
a few months later, in Chapeltown, we did,
breaking through the cops' cordon and piling
into the parade of sieg-heiling boneheads,
Sikhs and 'West Indians' fighting beside us,
dragging loud-hailered Webster from the back
of his PA-ed flatback, putting in the boot:
Black and white – unite and fight.

2. Trigger

The back wall
of Harrow Street's outside lavs,
a blank red-brick canvas
facing the cop-shop,
where punk-legend
'that' Billy Johnson emulsioned
THE POLICE KILLED BLAIR
in square letters three foot high.
(He'd intended to paint BLAIR *PEACH*,
but ran out of wall.)
Blair Peach: teacher,
activist, man of letters:
NUT, ANL, SWP.

A St. George's Day rally
in the heart of Sikh Southall,
NF freedom of speech/intimidation
underwritten by the council
and the Special Patrol Group,
who clubbed Peach to death
and left his body on the street.
Eight thousand Sikhs
paid their respects at his open coffin.

A year or so later
on Harehills' immigrant streets,
we were jumped by British Movement skins
as we tore down their posters
near the Fforde Green pub.
Protecting my face,
I was gashed in the palm
by a broken bottle,
as we fought for our lives
in a running skirmish
along Roundhay Road.

At school on Monday,
I wore that scar with pride.
But I wasn't the weekend's
only casualty:
Gelderd-Ender Mick Grant
was sporting a proper shiner.

Q. How'd you get that, Mick?
A. Fighting niggers in Leeds.

> *TRIGGER!*
> *TRIGGER!*
> *TRIGGER!*
>
> *Shoot that nigger!*
> *Which nigger?*
> *That nigger!*
>
> *TRIGGER!*
> *TRIGGER!*
> *TRIGGER!*

NF, BM. Column 88.
Elland Road was like a Klan Rally.

3. Etcetera

Great Britain impoverished to post-war prosperity:
everyone working, but nobody earning and nothing
to buy. Capital needed labour for its unsocial
dirty work, but the natives wouldn't shift or shovel shit.

Jamaica & sub-continent took up the White Man's Burdens.
Race-rioting Teds, half-devil and half-child; Mosley,
that infantile Satan, master of puppets. Elite psychology
of fascism: malleable masses dependably deployable in the service
of their masters, to know – and keep – their place. *Send them back!*

Roman foreboding largely unwarranted. It naturalised
to jargon – multi-cultural, multi-ethnic, multi-faith –
and reality on the ground, common humanity working
its warmcockle nostrums. People simply got used to it,
to each other, cordially embracing, ignoring or hating.
A provisional peace of geniality and ghettos,
subject to periodic eruption. I was born to this.
The young know nothing else. This is England.

4. Mrs Duffy

You can't say anything about the immigrants...
all these eastern Europeans... where are they flocking from?

Gillian Duffy, in televised exchanges with Prime Minister Gordon Brown as
he campaigned for re-election in Rochdale, April 2010.

That was a disaster ... she was a sort of bigoted woman.

Gordon Brown's subsequent characterisation of Mrs Duffy to his aides,
inadvertently transmitted to journalists via the lapel microphone he was
wearing.

Wife, mother, grandmother: *bigot*.
special-needs carer,
thirty years' service: *bigot*.
Window-cleaner's daughter,
mother a mill-girl: *bigot*.
Life-long Labour, roots going deep;
the Red Flag at the Free Trade Hall,
the Rochdale Co-op, husband
and father red-raggers in the union.
(that's where she gets it from,
her 'forthright assertiveness'): *bigot*.
A white, working-class woman
from the hard-pressed, noble,
neglected and patronised North,
worried debt and her town's long decline,
jobs and her grandkids' futures: *bigot*.

Some things just can't be said. Even raising
the issue, in Blunkett's words, is 'bordering
on the fascist' – *bigot*. Self-censorship
gagged me just thinking this poem. Conspiracy
and politics: Labour 'opened the floodgates'
to 'rub the right's nose in diversity'
and stuff the ballots with 'ethnic' votes,
aided and abetted by the CBI,
keen to keep the dole queues pumped

to cow workers, break unions,
lower wages – and increase profits.
Three million unemployed. Three million
immigrants in the last ten years. The siren voice
of the BNP: *coming over here, taking our jobs*
(coming over here, scrounging on the dole).
The racist right, peddling fear and hate.
Immigration transcending itself, becoming
the touchstone issue for an frightened people
bewildered by change and bereft of identity.
Mrs Duffy's elegy for Rochdale –
the shops are closed, the markets gone, no jobs –
an elegy for working class England.
But it's not just the economy, stupid,
but the way we've come to live; separate,
uncommunitied, reduced to consumer
and lifestyle niches – virtual solipsists.
The communal culture that celebrates 'us'
usurped by the privatised 'I'.
There was never a Golden Age, but even
in *this* place, before cars and cable
and touch-screen's slavery, Tory darkness
and New Labour's false dawn, there was life
and thriving, a thronged high street and market,
cinemas, a theatre, libraries, pubs and teams.
In less than half a lifetime, almost everything's
gone, the stranded poor picking bargain-bin
bric-a-brac on Oxfam, fast-food streets.
Each man indoors before his screen, not knowing
his neighbour. The monied commute to work
and malls. Their suburbs could be anywhere.
Politicians in thrall to globalised capital,
peddling cynical yes-we-can dreams:
stuffing their pockets, building pensions and careers.
Big warehouses on the bypass, part-time,
short-time, casualised working, unsocial shifts,
low pay. Poles, Kurds and Ghanaians.
Bringing us back to where we started.

Sixty three million people on iPhones.
Malls and windfarms, HS2.
Suburbs sprawling over forests and fields
from which we feed and breathe.

Who are we? And how do we want to live?

5. The Transmigratory Soul of Muhammad Siddique Khan

The transmigratory soul of Muhammad Siddique Khan,
incarnate in the elephant cavalry
of world-seizing Jahangir and pitiless
Aurangzeb's claw of disembowelling,
passed from this world to the orgasmic
boudoir, bhang and French wine in an orchard
of mangoes, seventy-two virginal houris
attendant: thus chained to the wheel
for rebirthings numbered as the beautiful
names of Allah, (al-Khafid, ar-Rafi).

The transmigratory soul of Muhammad Siddique Khan
quickening in the Hindoo womb seeded
in the service of Angrezi Sahibs
intriguing against the Nizam of Hyderabad:
strangled at birth, dug under the dust
of the midnight peepal, enlightened
out of graveyard earth by Durga's dirt pariahs;
reborn as sabred-sepoy, sealing those Sahibs
into Kali-Ghat's death-hole, drawing down
karmic justice: quartering by cannon.

The transmigratory soul of Muhammad Siddique Khan,
votary-vehicled in Ranjit's rainbow-Punjab;
a fakir vending charms for alms. Vatula,
vyakula, sainted congener of sadhus
and swamis, bosomed to Ind as health,
wealth and merit. To the Sahibs, nought
but a lousy beggar; to the Mullahs,
kufr, a shaitan of shirk, usurper
of Allah, (al-'Ahad, al-Hafiz). Khost
claimed him: death by typhoid and Pashtunwali.

The transmigratory soul of Muhammad Siddique Khan
became carnal in the khalsa's turbanned khaki,
the rifled corpse-pile in the Jallianwala garden.
One million Indian Muslims, banking
the King's Shilling. The plunder box closed
and graveyards opened. Allah, al-Mumit,
Shiva, destroyer of worlds. Wagah's fugue
bellicosity grieving Mahatma,
Jinnah's brute bifurcation crudely blaspheming
Kimball O'Hara's panentheist tawhid.

The transmigratory soul of Muhammad Siddique Khan
warps from Mirpur's whirring wheels to looming
Leeds: the Paki-bashing heartland of the heartless
West Riding. Three generations: *keep-your-head-
down-and-get-on-with-it, fit-in-we're-English-now,*
and *Allahu-akhbar*. All three simultaneous;
the same households; the same *heads*. Brothers
chasing brown. Brazilian G-string sisters.
Sarfraz Najeib, prone on the pavement outside
Majestyk, bleeding from the heel-print in his face.

The transmigratory soul of Muhammad Siddique Khan,
dutiful son, husband and father,
mortgagee, volunteer, teaching assistant,
role model Muslim and 'nice young man',
re-evaluates English existence.
Who am I? What am I doing here?
The Markazi Masjid has the answers
to these questions, culminating in,
*Your democratically elected
governments continuously perpetuate*

atrocities against my people
all over the world and your support
of them makes you directly responsible,
just as I am directly responsible
for protecting and avenging my Muslim brothers
and sisters. Until we feel security,
you will be our targets. And until you stop
the bombing, gassing, imprisonment
and torture of my people we will not stop this fight.
We are at war and I am a soldier.

The transmigratory soul of Muhammad Siddique Khan
is lashed to the wheel for seven times seventy
rebirths; tigers of Sunderbans, lions
of Gir, Istishhad's posturing peacocks.
Allah, al-Hasib, ar-Rahim. The sins
of the fathers are visited on the sons
to the third and fourth generations.
This is to be expected. Germany's Jews
were the most assimilated in Europe;
Rome's expelled for constant riot.

　　　　Dark horizon, some winter tree. Dark bird
　　　　bunched on the topmost bough. Stay a while
　　　　and share the vision: name both bird and tree.

The Song of the Yellowhammer

Æthelstan, war-wager   waster of wapentakes
humbler of hundreds   corpser of kings.
Albion passes   to Ælfred's wolf-whelp
abaser of armies   Lord of lives and lands.
Even the paths   of the Highland deer
belong to Ælle's   golden-haired Ætheling.

Egil Skallagrimson,
Egil's Saga

I

The yellowhammer's song
is the princeliest ditty
of Deira's summer buntings,
far surpassing schoedinus's
reedy flat battery
and the loose change rattle
of the corn, proclaiming
its paupered promise:
a little bit of bread and no cheese.

From the starveling clays of Lent
to the Mass of St. Michael's
stubblefield plenty,
the copsed and coverted
arable hedge-lands resound
with the scribbler's wheezing
demotic, sprig-summited
from barebone quick,
foaming may, shot-hard unripened haws.

Geolu ammer, tongue
of the pale-haired
Frisian barbarians,
Hengist and Horsa
of the wyverned-skin,
sons of Wictgils, son of Witta,
son of Wecta, son of Wotan,
sire of Thunor,
hammer of Hrungnir, daughter of Earth.

The Danelaw clays
are streaked with beaten gold.
Below the plough
the citrine ingas blows.
The byways are verged
with travelling ragwort,
sunakai, salno.
Lion's teeth blaze
from the field's rough fleece, seeded from the sun.

The ceorls of Wessex
are satisfied
with their crust and honour
not the ploughman.
Humber's plate is empty.
Tees and Medway, discontent.
A wind from the East,
the blown dunes fray:
cadent citronella from candled gorse.

II

The dragon-prowed fleet
of Ivar the Boneless
floats moored on Humber
like a raft of garefowl.
Squinted by blizzarding
Baltic snow, flailed foam
and strafing sand:
the bleached eyes of Ælle,
King of Northumbria, watching from the point.

Ravenspurn's
wind-whipped strandline.
Hood-stripped
bare-tonsured
becloaked
as wandering Wotan,
Wilgils gathers driftwood
in the wintry broken rose:
tumbling petals of schneeammer falling.

The white-tailed eagle's
sunlit eye
tracks Humber's gullet,
along Ouse, Don and Ea,
to the slow blonde stones
and saffron clays of Hampole.
An orchard
of yellow pears.
Aureate moon, soft light of xanthic tallow.

Worn and dislocate,
kelts ground on gravels
in the vale below the priory,
shredding their rainbows.
Suffocate gapes
and gasping gills
give out.
Kite and corvid,
horn-billed erne, sparring on the shoals.

III

Beck-walk from Hampole
to Holywell Wood
in a back-ripping tunnel
of hawthorns. Unbelieved
fish, fleeing upcurrent
before us: pike and barbel, chub.
And in a man-deep plunge-pool,
Hung in a sunshaft
column of light, a trout flicked its tail   vanished.

Whence the sturgeon?
Its English redds lie occluded,
occult. A seven-foot 'vagrant',
forked bankside at Towton,
armoured flanks
packed with hard caviare.
Others, exhaust kelts perhaps,
found floating bankside at Barnby Dun
and Bolham-on-Idle: stoned by frightened farmboys.

Mercian Sabrina,
Offa's moated failsafe,
Silts glutted with styria
from Purton to Tewkesbury,
to stone-bottomed Vrnwy and Tanat beyond.
At Oswestry's guffawing table
the simultaneous interpretation
of Cadwallon and Penda,
stripping the plate, unbuckling the bones, cleaving the noble jowl.

Æthelstan rests
in Aldhelm's Abbey
jowled by cheek
of the Naked Gardeners.
Eden fallen to satyric Arcadia
couched in celebrity We-Sex,
E-Sex, the only way,
South and Middle seaxe,
vortexing to Wen. The Saxons knew no North.

IV

Thunor at forge,
poaching gold
in the bellowing furnace.
Then the overhead malletings
of Mjollnir the helm-splitter,
shaping rings to deal in hall.
The song from clashing metals
shrills across the heath,
auric fletchings from the anvil, fleeing to the gorse.

Coney-cropped common
flaming with furze
from Hague Hall to Hargate.
In the yellowhammer's glebe
Ebenezer in exile dreamed
the People's Anthem:
ten English acres, neither thrones
and crowns - nor masters' drop-hammers
slamming and sparking, exploding men like bombs.

From Biggin Hill to Church Fenton
the arable aches with song,
ploughmen and pilots
raising tankards in the taverns
until dusk throbs crimson
from the cities of the west.
Broad-winged spitfires
sputtering home, break
the anxious reverie, screaming squadrons of June's dark swifts.

White cliffs lidded
with wheat and whin,
gull-wheeled and flakked with jackdaws.
Demobbed from Burma
to a prefab on the Vale
and life on the Barnsley seam,
Eck trudges sludge to Frickley pit
in dawn's drowsing serenade.
The unknown familiar song. Those birds were never blue.

The heavy horse
of Wink House farm no more.
The plovered pastures
put to plough,
now forested in rape.
The gorsy commons scoured
to muck and agrochemical brass.
Feast and field-folk, banished.
Golden lads and lasses, pissing petals in the wind.

Lehman Brothers
Kardashian sisters:
the loue of money is the root of all euill.
Whore is to body
as slave is to labour
and celebrity to soul.
In each case, ker-ching.
Three card mounte-
bank conmen, conjuring profits and total loss.

Breath of plug-in air-freshener,
suffocate central heating.
Tight shoes and top button.
Door-car-door return.
Podged, paralytic, stinking
of lipids and anxious with cancer.
Xmas, Valentine's –
many happy returns. We escape
to nature like a drowning man surfacing, before going under again.

The tumblestone cottage
at Hampole Wood,
bramble derelict,
shooting blackthorn.
Chop bones, horseshoes, residual brassicas.
The woodcocked rides
now clotted with pheasant.
Keepers fishing for fur with nooses.
Tractors trawling the oceaned arable with baleen of steel.

Cut the vines
from the hoary crabtree;
plank the pens against the fox;
birth milk and mutton
in backyard barn and byre.
To each man his allotment.
With plough-turned fieldstone
gentled hands will build
once more, and lift the lintels of long tumbled halls.

A fair field full of folk,
the stooked crofts of Ringstone
via Scawsby's red pikes
and daggered Mile End.
The frosted fallows
of Frickley's Winter Palace,
stormed with driven hares:
blasted bloodless by yeoman grapeshot,
the truncheons of Orgreave, St. Peter's cutlassed field.

Bismarck's maxim
following Clausewitz.
Divisions make it so.
Stalin shrank not
from exemplary slaughter
and made a New World: ditto Hitler,
Truman, buck-toothed Saloth Sar.
Too much blood, I can't commit.
Not Samuel, but Jeremy, cursed of God; a prophet.

                    V

Fafnir at Gnitaheath,
smug in his cavern of gorse,
curls his coils
around Otter's Ransom.
At the place where water springs forth,
Sigurd unsheaths
flame-edged Gram.
The incomprehensible
screethings of yellowhammers relay across the moor.

Sigurd hacked out
the worm's black heart
with the anvil-cleaving blade.
Fafnir's dying benediction:
'Gold will be your death'.
Indeed, through greed
all men are monstered,
but in blood is lore
and shriving. The dripping clot spitted, turning over fire.

Dusk-camped under piebald birches,
the inscrutable song
of the yellowhammer
throbs in the gloaming
like a raw sore.
Drawn by the cook fire's golden glow,
chattering nuthatches spiral down:
Regin sleeping, Sigurd licking
from fingers pink froth foamed from Fafnir's broiling heart.

The pricked ears of the man-wolf
opened on Gnitaheath
to language of birds,
the spite of nuthatches, sharp-faces
turned to earth and advantage, urging
betrayal and accumulation –
enrich yourself kill friendship and honour
slay the one that trusts- like fishwives,
or lawyers, disinheriting children, picking the pockets of corpses.

In the King's tent at Vin-Heath
Egil hung up his harp.
And the song of the yellowhammer
sounded over the hazelled field
like a skald in hall:
you are the people in the land
know you are the people
know it is your land.
Shield-wall bristling with halberds, tusked like the eofor.

Acknowledgements

Some of the poems in this book first appeared in the following magazines, journals, books and anthologies: *Dwang 3, Black Herald Review, Hearing Voices, The Stinging Fly, The Tablet, Cake, Hamilton Stone Review, The Morning Star, Hinterland* and *Digging the Seam, Popular Cultures of the 1984/5 Miners' Strike.* 'Objective One' won the *Raise Your Banners Political Poetry Competition* in 2009. 'The Battle of Brunanburh' is a homage to Geoffrey Hill's *Mercian Hymns.* A verse of the Dropkick Murphys' version of Ed Pickford's 'Workers' Song' is quoted in 'Scum of the Earth' (page 52), as is a generally suppressed verse of Cecil Frances Alexander's popular hymn, 'All Things Bright and Beautiful' (page 55). A couplet from Morrissey's 'Irish Blood, English Heart' is quoted in the poem named for that song (page 168). Ed Reiss helped improve some of the poems via his comments on a draft copy of the manuscript.